THE ILLUSTRATED HISTORY OF THE WORLD

-With Pictures-

taken from the pages of

The Big Shiny Thing in the Sky

by

DAVID ROWE

PAUL WATKINS
STAMFORD
1990

Published by
PAUL WATKINS
18 Adelaide Street,
Stamford,
Lincolnshire, PE9 2EN

ISBN 1 871615 17 8 (Hard cover)
ISBN 1 871615 18 6 (Soft cover)

Thanks Ann and Shaun

Design, Layout & Typesetting
by the author
and
Donkey Industries
Dôlhaidd isaf,
Castell Newydd Emlyn,
Dyfed SA38 9HU.

Original illustrations by
Ann Votikas

Picture credits to the
Murray Wren Picture Library

Photoset by A.L.Publishing Services

Printed and bound by
Woolnoughs Bookbinding,
Irthlingborough, Northamptonshire.

INTRODUCTION

Thought: Blessed are the poor in spirit, for they shall be truly screwed.

Once upon a time men lived in the tops of banana trees, grunting "Smash the Scum!" if any male came too close, jumping up and down thumping their chests, jabbering "What a lovely pair!" if any female came close.
Over the years things progressed a little. Slowly language, and thus thought, became more refined, and men became more intelligent. They remained obsessed with attacking one another, and with mammary glands, but they did manage to tame the horse, to play the violin, to invent algebra and to write poetry. Slowly man edged down his tree.
Over these same years man also acquired money and/or a soul and/or a vote, and soon some men were busy trying to wrest these things from their fellows. Various methods were used, but none were altogether satisfactory: those that were effective -burning at the stake, throwing to the lions, beheading, shooting, etc- were rather terminal, and by decreasing the number of men, they decreased the supply of money and/or souls and/or votes available in the future. If less positive methods were used, man was intelligent enough to hang on to his possessions. This problem thwarted the dreams of kings, politicians and zealots throughout history.

The solution was eventually found by an impressive example of lateral thinking: instead of trying to take things against man's will, if you took away his will, then he would simply give you what you wanted.
Sunspeak was thus invented: a fiendish ruse that erodes the intelligence of any man exposed to it. This diabolical device was used in an adult comic which men were induced to read by various devilish means.
By disguising its primitive grunts and jabberings as real language, **Sunspeak** deprives man of language, and thus of thought.
Sunspeak was an astounding success. Soon there were millions reading it, unknowingly performing this do-it-yourself lobotomy. Soon these millions were happily giving away their money and/or souls and/or votes as directed. Slowly language became less refined. Slowly man clambered back up his tree.
Now **Sunspeak** is everywhere, for success has spawned imitators. What would life be like if **Sunspeak** had not been invented? How would we know exactly what colour knickers exactly which princess wore? Would we be able to understand politicians who said things like "We hold these truths to be self-evident, that all men are created equal, that they are endowed by their Creator with certain unalienable Rights, that among these are Life, Liberty and the pursuit of Happiness", rather than those whose empty words and flashy slogans convey their empty, flashy hectoring? Would life not be too intolerably tedious if we did not know that Mrs Arbuthnot's cat could fart the first two lines of God Save the Queen in perfect tune?
But what would life be like if **Sunspeak** had been invented earlier? Would we be different in a world where Jehovah had not said "I am the Lord thy God ... Thou shalt have no other gods before me." but "Jo-Jo goes it alone!!!"; where it was not said of Cleopatra that "age cannot wither her, nor custom stale her infinite variety", but that she had a "double aspect, big frontage, in a sought-after location"; where things had not started with "In the beginning God created the heaven and the earth", but with "Big G. Turns It On" and "Phew!"

Continued on Page Four

The Big Shinything in the Sky

ANSWERS TO LAST WEEK'S QUIZ

ON PAGE 11

Date: Day 6 | Price: One apple core | Thought: Rome wasn't built in a day

BIG G TURNS IT ON!

AND IT'S A SCORCHER!

Yes, folks, it's here at last and right bang on time! This morning, Big G, looking tired after his epic six-day workout, gave a big grin, stroked his long white beard, turned to our reporter **RUDEPRATT MUDROCK,** and said, **"Well, R. M., I think that'll do. Let's give it a whirl!"**

Big G, the infinitely-old, white-haired initiator of this creation-job scheme, grinned cheekily and then said in his booming voice, "The first three days were a bit boring, if the truth was told. I guess I was just getting my eye in. Night and day, land and sea, grass and trees. And a few herbs to season," he added with a jocular wink.

TO RULE THE WORLD

But day 4 really lit up the world! **THE BIG SHINY THING IN THE SKY** appeared. "It just came to me in a flash," Big G said. "Something to rule the day. Now I've got to find a name for it. Scrotum? Anaglypta? Walsall?" he mused.

"Hang on, Big G," our doughty reporter said, "I've got an idea that could make our fortunes. Let's have a competition. Readers send in their suggestions with a fiver and there's a prize for the winner, something really good, like immortality, or ..."

"But I haven't created reading yet," Big G said glumly.

"Never mind. We'll just use little words. And lots of pictures. You'll see. Believe in me. This could be the start of something big. And there's something else: do you remember that spare rib thing you had left over? Well, it's giving me real gip stuck in my side, and I've had this really super idea. I wondered if you could perhaps have a go at ..."

"My God," said Big G with a sigh, "I've no sooner finished making it than you're complaining. If I hear any more out of you, then I'll create

(continued on page three)

WHAT WILL HE DO ON DAY 7?

Will he create Match of the Day??
Will he create an omnibus edition of Eastedeners?
Mysterious ways fully explained on page 11.

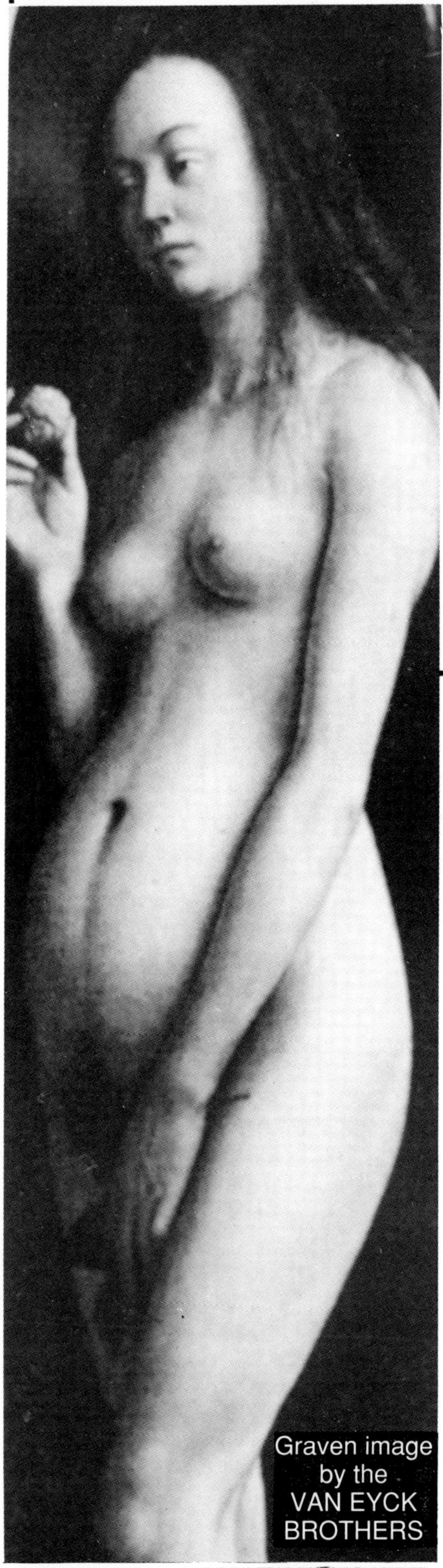

Graven image by the VAN EYCK BROTHERS

WOW

NOW THAT'S WHAT WE CALL SPARE RIB! ———

If our local takeaway served spare rib like this little beauty, we'd be down there every day, but we wouldn't bother with the greens, would we, fellas?
EVErything in the garden's blooming lovely!!!
We couldn't believe our luck when we saw who had moved in next door. We can tell you we'll be around to offer a right neighbourly welcome as soon as possible.
As they say, **EVE**rybody needs good neighbours.
We're just hoping that Big G gets round to creating autumn soon!!!

PLUS

KINKY KRAZE SERPENTS ARE IN SEE PAGE 7

PLUS PLUS PLUS

NO THUGS IN EDEN!

Neanderthal Man banished to Millwall!
Full, horrifying details of Homo Millwallianis on p. 9.

DISASTER ON DAY 6

CREEPING THINGS CREATED

PLUS PLUS PLUS

Super Prizes in the Super Creation Competition
Find a Name for the Big Shiny Thing in the Sky

THE BIG S

1001 FUN THINGS TO DO WITH THE KIDS ON A WET DAY

Date: ||||| ||||| ||||| ||||| ||||| ||||| ||||| ||||| ||||| ||||| ||||| ||||| ||||| ||||| ||||| ||||| ||||| ||||| ||||| ||||| ||||| ||||| ||||| ||||| ||||| ||||| ||||| ||||| ||||| || Er... I've lost count! Price: 1 pair of galoshes Thought: Every cloud has a silver lining

ARK ARK

Well, yes, perhaps it should be a cuckoo, not a lark!

600-year-old good life loony Noah is at it again! An ark! he said. I want to build an ark!

YOU CAN'T GET THE WOOD, YOU KNOW!

"Gopher wood," he told our reporter, "that's the only thing for arks." We can just see the faces at the local d-i-y store! "I think I'll make it a good size," said Noah, "about 300 cubits by 50 ought to do." Yes, can you imagine it? He's taking all the family and their pets as well.

And until you've seen Noah's front room, you've no idea what it means to have pets!!!

He'll be fine as soon as he realises that the water should be outside the ark!!!
Mind you, he's enjoying himself, and we wouldn't mind paddling that little craft, would we, fellas? You'd just need to watch out for the sap rising!!!

MR AND MRS NOAH TRYING TO INVENT NAVIGATION!

SEE OUR SUPER BIG S SOGGY SUMMER FUN-FILLED SPECIAL

IT'S A GONNA RAIN, CHILDREN

Weathermen boob again!

We don't know why they bother! They're never right. Sun cream and parasols and everybody to the beach, they promised.
Ha! Ha! And just look at it now!!

Rain! Rain! Rain!
It's every year the same. The school holidays start, down it comes.
God knows what we've done to deserve this!

EVEN THE DUCKS HAVE HAD ENOUGH

See "The Big S. says" on page 5

WHAT A LARK!!!

HAVE TO ALTER THE DOOR A BIT

Noah admitted today that he had made a few mistakes with the doors!

He plans to make them a bit bigger one of these days because they can't get Rex, the family's pet dinosaur, in.
"We couldn't bear to leave him in kennels," quipped Mrs Noah gaily, "while we all go swanning off. Oh! Excuse me a minute," she said as she hurried to get the washing off the line, "it looks as if it's coming on to rain."

TOURIST BOOM COLLAPSES.

The terrible weather is ruining the tourist trade, just as things were picking up after the catastrophic loss of the Garden of Eden franchise.
Mount Ararat is doing well, but all other locations are a right wash-out!
Our photo of the promenade at Baghdad yesterday shows just how bad things are!
If only theme parks had
(continued on page 13)

The Prom at Baghdad

THE BIG S

Make sure you're not left waiting for it!

Date: Still pretty dark, but quite warm for the time of year. Price: One virgin
Thought: Virgin on the ridiculous.

Place a regular order with your newsagent now!

GIVE 'EM A WASH AND PUT 'EM TO WORK!!!

An unruly mob of long-haired, dirty people, probably from Millwall, tried to crash in on the super fun mid-summer Big S celebrations at Stonehenge yesterday.

"I mean," said the Archdruid, "it's just not on. They didn't even bring their own virgins! This is a serious business, and we can't allow

(continued on page 4)

A Super Fun New and Exciting Big S Series:

GREAT RELIGIONS OF THE WORLD

Part One: Druidism.

How do you sacrifice a virgin? Archdruid tells all on page 5.

WAITING FOR IT

Archdruids, druids and a bevy of beautiful virgins were out before dawn yesterday waiting for it!

- - And there were quite a few anxious faces in the crowd, we can tell you!

RM TOUCHED

Anybody who is anybody was there at the world's greatest construction waiting for the world's greatest event: the arrival of the Big S!!!

Rudepratt Mudrock, supreme archdruid, said he was touched that so many loyal friends had turned up and hoped they all had a good time.

Yes, folks, was it really the shortest night of the year, or did it just seem that way with all that lovely stuff-as-dreams-are-made-on hanging around waiting for it?

BIG S MIDSUMMER SACRIFICE SPECIAL

Fun things to do with mistletoe

Don't let that smile let you down at your community mid-summer sacrifice.

See our **Big S Special offer** on page 7

Who Boobed this time?

Heart-broken mother of 12 tells the terrible secret -IN HER OWN WORDS AND WITH PAINFUL INTIMATE DETAILS- of how she was nearly sacrificed by mistake.

Get the Big S. Summer Solstice Special!

THE BIG S

Date: Well, some say 1491 b.c., others about 700 b.c.
Price: One timbrel
Thought: Keep on taking the tablets, Momo.

Amnesty on graven images

Hand them in to your local tabernacle now.

Guaranteed no stonings

COVETING ASSES IS OUT

Crackdown on law and order

New laws proposed

698-year-old party-pooper Moses came down off his hill yesterday and spilt the beans. He told our reporter that there was going to be a major shake-up in the laws, and that strict new measures were to be taken to cut out idolatry, adultery, perjury, murder, stealing, swearing, coveting and pretty much everything else that seemed to be fun.

But you've got to do something to relax after a hard day's wandering in the wilderness. **And picking up manna and following a pillar of smoke is not what today's kids want.**

They've even had to cancel the match on Sunday between the Levites and the Edomites. It would be much better if they

(continued on page 7)

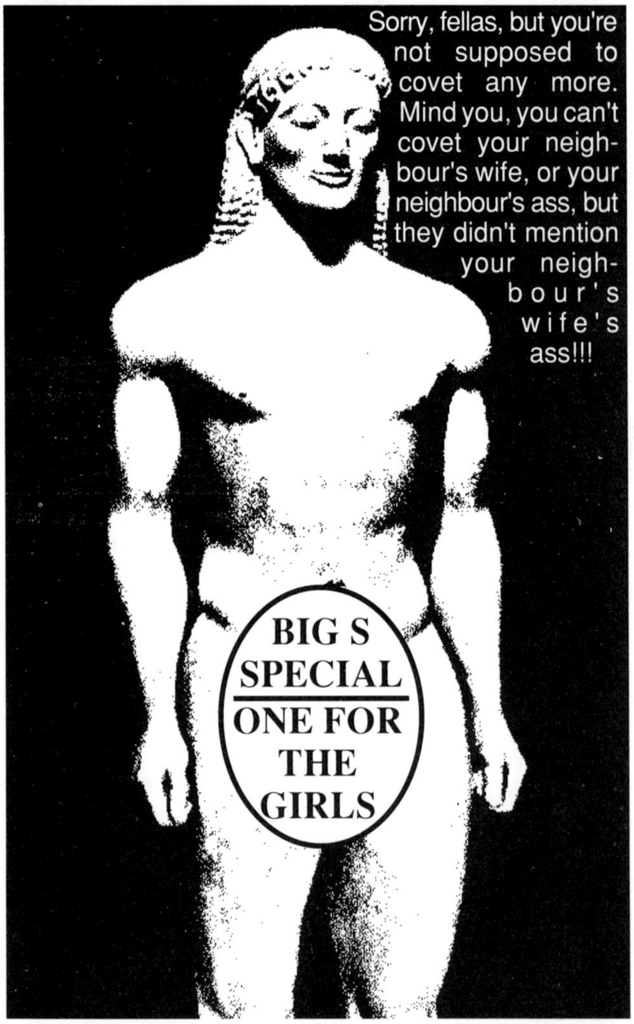

The Big S says this will put the kids back on the streets

Hittites? Shittites! The Pharaoh will knock 'em for six!

PLAY FAIR, PHARAOH!!!

Wouldn't you like her as your little sister? Nefertiti would certainly get my sibling sparks sizzling. But she doesn't do a thing for playboy brother and fiancé Prince Ramses! He's put the wedding off yet again, saying he's got a terrible headache!

RAMSES SHAMSES IN EXCEST OUTRAGE

But while he won't make an honest woman of little sis, we know who he **has** been playing around with behind the Pyramids, and he's not even a cousin!

The Big S says it's time to do your bit, Ram the Sham.

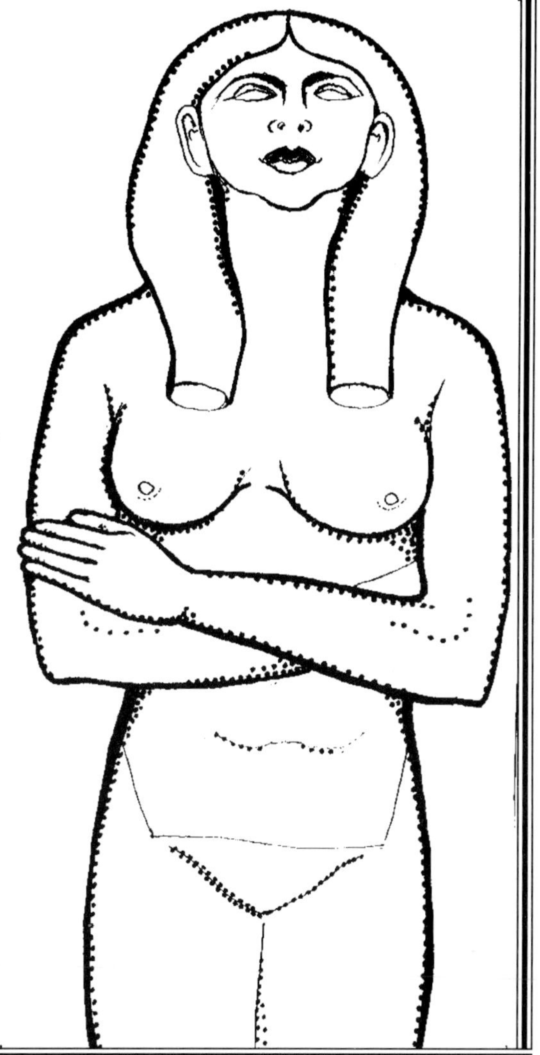

Second in our exciting series Great faiths of the World: Judaism!!!

- What to do if you smite out your man-servant's tooth!
- Is the price for enticing a maid that is not betrothed and lying with her too high?

WIN YOUR DREAM TOMB!

see page 8.

Cookery:

THIS WEEK'S GREAT FREE RECIPE

Pig's trotters in jelly

- GIVE 'EM A WASH AND PUT 'EM TO WORK!!!

That's what the Big S says to the whiners and the scroungers and the hand-out experts who've been taking, taking, taking ever since they got out of Egypt!
We don't suppose they helped part the waters of the Red Sea! Too busy running for it, we bet! Then it was water! Give us water, they whined. And they got water. Then it was bread! Give us bread, they whinged. And they got bread! Now it's quails! Sitting on their back-sides in their tents in the middle of the desert, expecting everything to drop from heaven into their greedy hands.

The Big S. says: this has gone far enough. Give 'em a wash and put 'em to work. And if they don't want to work, put 'em in the army.
These namby-pamby, liberal, pinko, limp-wristed social worker poofters with their personal filorock organisers and their portable (cont page 5)

Big S. SPORT! Angel of death 3457 Egypt 0. Hebrews in sending-off shocker.

THE BIG S

ROYAL FAMILY SPECIAL

Date: The Calends Price: 1 Greek urn Thought: If at first you don't succeed, troy, troy, troy again

HELEN HOPS OFF TO PARIS

EXCLUSIVE ROYAL BIG S

AGAMEMNON'S NEW INVENTION

King Aggie is riding a new hobby-horse this week. Last week, as we reported in our Big S Super Royal Story Exclusive, he invented a new and exciting technique to make a likeness of himself. "You just take a large sheet of gold, put it over your head, lie down and beat yourself in the face with a small hammer. It's quite good really," said Aggie, "a pretty good likeness. But I had to give it up in the end. I found that I couldn't enjoy my food after a couple of hours of steady hammering, and the nosebleeds were getting embarrassing."

Special Royal Report

TROUBLE WITH THE WIND

Menelaus cursed at Aulis. King Aggie and Princess Iphie plan Bar-B-Que to cheer up Moody Monarch. Queen Clytemnestra wishes Aggie many happy returns!

You could launch my ship any time you like, Helen. I could just fancy being piped aboard this little craft, couldn't you, fellas?

Would you be upset if your wife went off to Paris for the weekend?

We can tell you that Menelaus was hopping mad when his wife hopped off!

"See if I care," he told our reporter, "I'm just getting these thousand ships together to go fishing with a few pals."

The Big S says : you don't fool us, Menelaus.

GOOSED BY ZEUS!

Yes, hell-cat Helen kept up the family tradition this weekend when she jumped on the last ferry for Troy.

No doubt she gets her habit of swanning off from her mother Leda who was well and truly goosed by Zeus when she wasn't looking!

"She's probably gone to do a bit of Calend shopping," sister Queen Clytemnestra lied bravely when questioned by our reporter at the palace. "Things are a little spartan at home, after all. I'm just lucky, I suppose, that I've got my little Agamemnon. At least I know that our love will last for ever and ever and ever and ever and ever and ever

(continued on page 7)

SPECIAL ROYAL STORY

GOPHER WOOD SECRET

"But," he shouted excitedly, "just imagine a horse that never eats, never drinks, never gets ill, never dies and never needs shoeing." Aggie claims to have managed all of that. Now he's working on getting it to move, but that shouldn't take long, he said this morning when we watched him putting his horse through its paces.

And it did look impressive! "It's all in the wood," he confided, as yet again he tried to lead the horse to water, (continued page 7)

Big S Sport: Aggie's new nag is our red-hot tip for the 3.30

THE BIG S

Date: Pharaz begat Hezron, and Hezron begat Ram, and Ram begat Amminadab, and Amminadab begat Salmon, and Salmon begat Boaz, and Boaz begat Obed, and Obed begat Jesse, and Jesse begat David and, my goodness, how time flies, he's already about so big.
Price: 5 smooth stones. Thought: The bigger they are, the harder they fall.

Jonathan tells all:
"We're just good friends! Daddy didn't mean to throw that javelin."
The Big S says: **page 9**

Royal Peeping Tom Exclusive

Peek-a-boo! We saw you

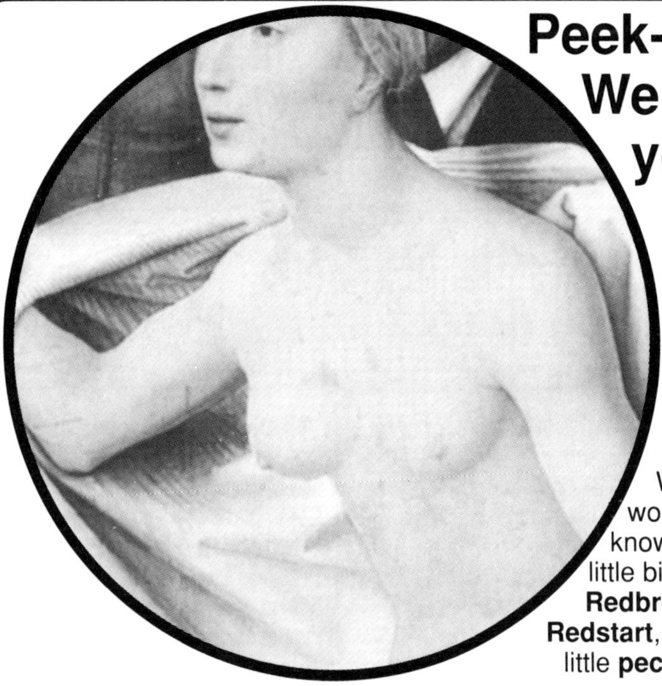

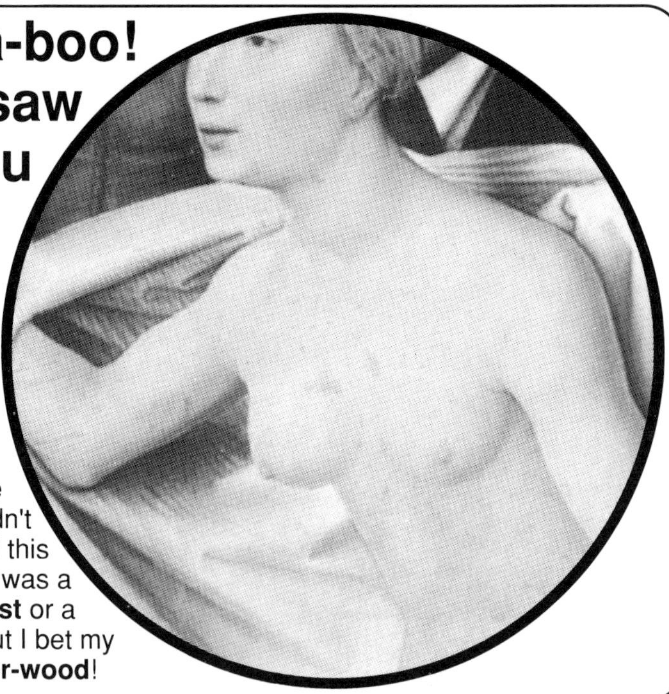

We wouldn't know if this little bird was a **Redbreast** or a **Redstart**, but I bet my little **pecker-wood**!

Time to get out of the Bath, Sheba

Local lovely was caught with her assets stripped when randy dandy Dave went up to the roof for a bit of bird-watching. Handsome shepherd hero, part-time giant basher and king has an ornithological bent, not to mention his bent ...
No, seriously, folks, he doesn't say no to a bit of bird-fancying when he's not too busy writing songs, or playing the harp at the Royal Command Performances. But he must have been surprised to get a right Royal eyeful of this little species! Makes us feel like rushing home and putting a bird-bath in our garden right now!
"I wasn't sure at first what it was," King David said. "I couldn't tell whether it was a Redbreast or a Blue
(continued on page three)

Men of the Moment: Exclusive Interviews

Today: Uriah the Hittite launches a campaign for increased personal hygiene.

The Big S says: Hittite? Shittite! You've got more than a spider in your bath, Uriah. Cleanliness begins at home!!!

GOTCHA GOLLY

Good Golly, Goliath, how are the mighty fallen

Giant grounded!

Handsome hero Dave the Rave took time off from watching the sheep yesterday to nip off to the battlefield to see how his brothers were doing, just as Goliath was throwing his weight around.

"Anybody fancy a scrap?" cried the Philistine.

By Jesse, he's a good little 'un

Huh," said David, "nobody kicks sand in my face." And with that he started off towards him.

"Hey, big mouth," he called out merrily and, whistling a snatch of his latest psalm, he bent down to

(continued on page 5)

SHOWBIZ SPECIAL

Dave's new ditty, "Hear me when I call", with "By the rivers of Babylon" on the B side, shoots to the top of the Judean charts.

GREAT COMPETITION

WIN A DATE WITH A PRINCESS

Answer the question "Who is the absolutely greatest, and we really mean the very, very greatest king in the whole world?"

In case you're finding that one a bit hard, we'll give you a clue: it begins with S, has four letters and he lives right here in Judea.

Send the answer on a Philistine foreskin and you could enter our great prize draw.

Full details page 11

THE BIG S

ROYAL FAMILY EXCLUSIVE

Hey, Sol, with 1000 wives, how come you've only got 16 kids?

Date: Too knackered to count. Price: One concubine Thought: Safety in numbers

KING LOVES STRANGE WOMEN

THE BIG S SAYS THAT'S PRETTY LOW IN THE BONKING AVERAGES!

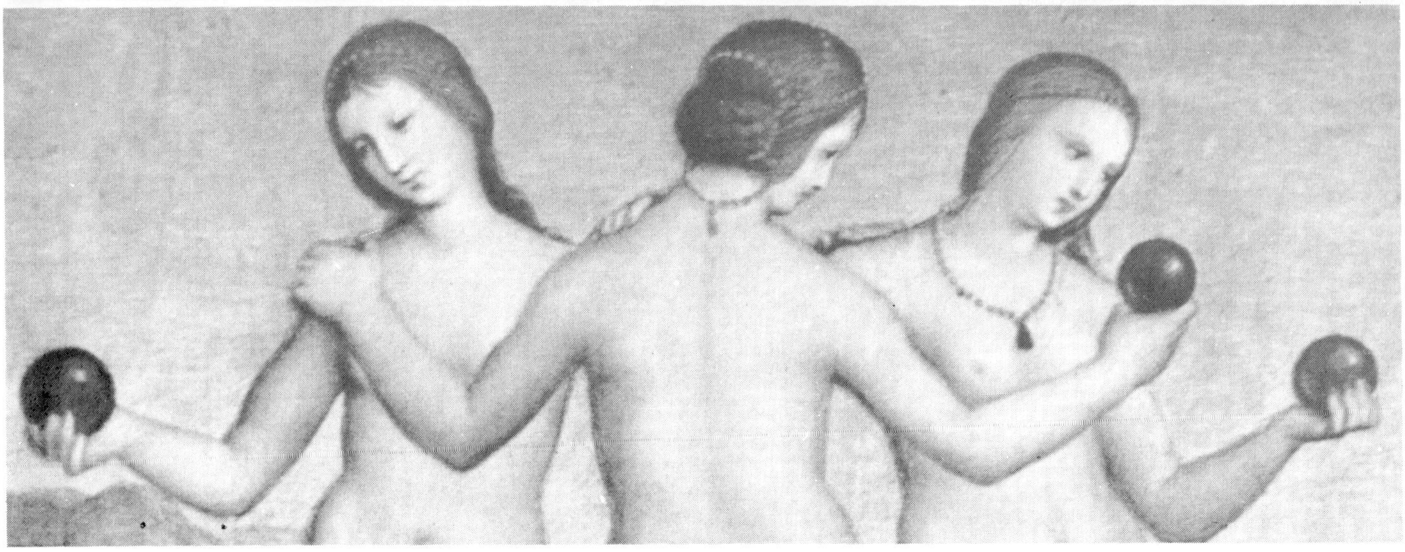

HITTITES BAN SOL'S SUPER NEW HIT SONG

King Solomon was outraged when he learnt that the Hittites had banned his new hit song!!!

"Damn cheek," he said as he led Lily, his latest bride and number 1000 in the list, from the temple this afternoon. "They just ain't got rhythm, ain't got no soul, those Hittites," he complained.
Mother Bathsheba smiled, "Yes, that's right, darling, and I should know because my first was a Hittite. He was always complaining when I used to sing in the bath."
"I mean," mumbled Solomon, "what's pornographic about goblets and fields of wheat and pomegranates and clusters of grapes? Some people have just got dirty minds."

"I am black, but comely."
Now that's what we call wisdom!
This little smartie can dance a nifty little hornpipe and could pass our OOOhh! level any time at all!

You've got to hand it to him, he certainly gets around a bit.
And, from what we hear, he **does** get it handed to him quite a lot. Daughters of Pharaohs, Moabites, Ammonites, Edomites, Zidonians and Hittites!!! That's what we call pretty catholic, and that's a pretty good trick for a Jewish king!!!
But Hittites? Did you have to, Sol?

THE BIG S SAYS: IS IT WISE, SOLOMON?
Yes, this week, King Solomon made it 1000 not out. And this is one royal collection that isn't open to the public!
Yes, folks, he's got 700 wives and 300 concubines, and that, we say, ought to be enough for any man.
The old proverb may well say that pheasants, partridges and princes should be well hung, but a wise man knows when to stop.

BONKING BY NUMBERS
On Wednesday he got hitched to a blushing Rose of Sharon, but by Thursday he had called out "Thank you, 999, your time is up," and off he raced to pick a little Lily of the valley to round off the thousand! We bet it's not sheep he counts when he can't get to sleep!

QUEEN OF SHEBA ARRIVES IN TOWN!

Queen of Sheba in town to host new series of Mastermind.

Solomon to answer on Judaic religion up to and including 950 b.c.

Great new prizes! Spices, precious stones and gold to be won!!!

The Big S says: The Hits are the Pits!
What about Freedom of Speech?

THE BIG S

Socrates' suicidal sip

The Big S says: it's a shame a few more poofs don't take the hint.
See page 5

Date: Confucius he say: time an illusion. Price:10 non-illusory drachmae Thought: It's all Greek to me

"SHE DOESN'T LOOK THAT OLD TO ME!"

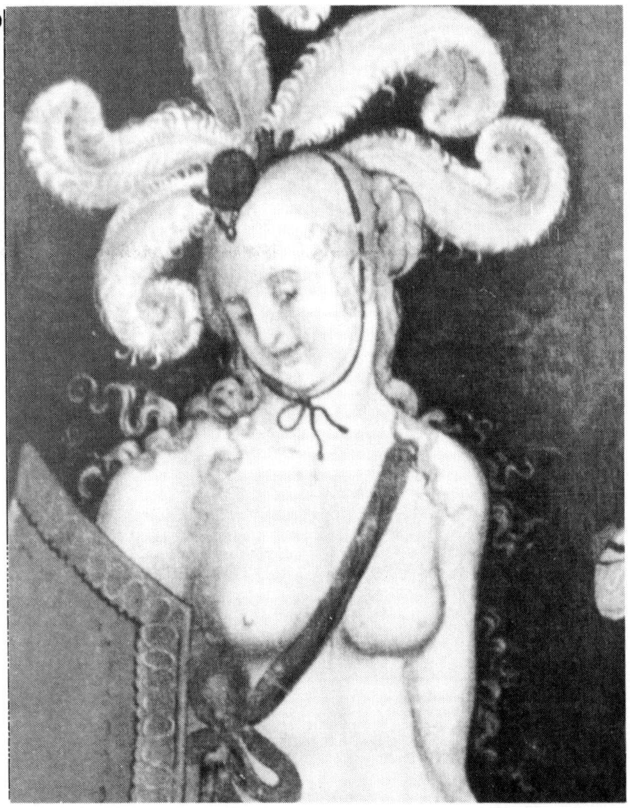

Handsome hero Oedipus fresh from outwitting the Sphinx, was married yesterday to lovely Queen Jocasta. Some malicious tongues have been saying that if Oedipus had seen Jocasta first, he might have preferred to be eaten by the Sphinx.

But odd-ball Oedipus seems well enough pleased. When questioned by our reporter, just as they were about to set off on their island-hopping honeymoon, he said "I wish you'd stop going on about it. You'd think she was old enough to be my mother, the fuss everybody's making. Besides, an older woman brings experience and maturity to a relationship. Can you imagine being married to one of those silly scroll three girls who just giggle and think of new togas and dabble in Sophist philosophy?"

The Big S says: take no notice, Oedipus. Just keep your eye on the ball.

THIRD IN EXCITING SERIES

GREAT RELIGIONS OF THE WORLD: CONFUCIANISM

More kinky sayings of Confucius, the latest loony-tune that's all the rage where the little yellow people live. See page 15.

FOREIGN NEWS

Plebs are revolting in Rome

The Big S says: Try living in Millwall!!! You wouldn't complain so much then.

No, seriously though, it does make a nice change from the Hittites, who have always been revolting.

See full details on page 13

UP AND ATOM, DEMO

NOW WE'VE HEARD IT ALL!

Democritus and a bunch of loony layabout friends say that everything is made up of little tiny bits whizzing around for ever!!!

THE BIG S SAYS: TRY AND KEEP IN THE SHADE FOR A WHILE, DEMO!

MORE SUPER BIG S ROYAL WEDDING EXTRA SPECIAL FUN PHOTOS INSIDE!!!

See pages 2,3,4,5,6,7,8,9,10,11,12,13,14,15,16,17,18.

WAR NEWS SPECIAL: Persians on the carpet again! They take another beating!!!

NO ROOF NO LOO

Tourists caught in holiday hotel rip-off scandal.

Holidaymakers in Greece this week were complaining bitterly about local conditions. Service was bad and some of the hotels were not even finished.

"Ours didn't even have a roof, or an inside lavvy," complained one Preston pensioner. "You wouldn't mind so much, but I paid extra to be right in the middle of town, and then they stick you up here on this bloomin' great hill. I thought Carthage was bad enough last year with all those elephants walking around. I ruined my new sandals."

Thousands have been terribly disappointed. "I wish there had been another chariot controllers' strike," a wealthy woad manufacturer from Dorset said. "I could have stayed at home and done the garden."

"Cradle of civilisation, my foot," complained one mother of 8 from Dublin, "they haven't even learned how to build proper yet. I've seen better roofs on our caves back home. It wouldn't surprise me if this dump is still like this in a thousand years."

A group of Millwall supporters was very upset: "There ain't nuffin worff smashin' up," one grunted, "somebody's been an' done it already."

THE BIG S

Date: Er, er, ... Price: Er, er, ... Thought: Be kind to dumb animals

As tasty a bit of wares as we've seen in many a long day at the fair. Perhaps he's not as simple as we think!

LITERARY BIG S-PLEMENT

WHAT A BORE!!!

Well, folks, they do say there's nowt so queer as folks, but you wouldn't believe what has hit the best-sellers list over in Greece! They're all agog at the new block-buster about some old Queen hundreds of years ago who sloped off to Paris for a bit on the side!

The Big S asks: What's the fuss?

The government's full of old queens who do the same **every** weekend!!!

The Big S says Go home, Homer! and take your Silly-ad with you!!!

SHOW-BIZ SPECIAL BIG S-PLEMENT

New song sensation shoots to the top!

Simple Samson met Delilah,
Going to the fair,
Said simple Samson to the damsel,
May I taste your wares?

GREAT NEW SUPER COMPETITION

Answer one simple riddle and win a whole new wardrobe of super fab gear!!!

SEE PAGE 11 FOR FULL, EXCITING DETAILS!

Samson delivering his after-dinner speech at a wedding!

OUR LOVE WILL LAST FOR EVER AND EVER AND EVER AND EVER

So said long-haired super-stud Samson as he was led from the temple yesterday.

"We are very much in love," said woman-about-town Delilah, smiling at her new live-in lover, Samson, the celebrated simpleton and 20-year-old part-time lion tamer. Samson, who is not totally unknown to the harlots of Gaza, met his wife when he was in town for a quick session of riddle-me-ree.

OUT OF THE STRONG

"I was a bit upset about that spot of bother down in Timnath," grunted Samson to our reporter yesterday, "but you lot from the press made a real meal of it. I only killed thirty, and some of them I hardly touched. It wasn't fair."

As he fretted he pulled a few stones from the temple wall which began to lean perilously. "Don't worry, darling," purred Delilah, "that's all over now. Let's slip along home for a nice spot of bondage."

THE BIG S

Date: 13 June, 33rd year of the reign
Price: A little round piece of gold with a picture on it.

Thought: Skydrops keep falling on his head

Pistil-packing would-be mommas given a cold shower!

BEGONIAS DON'T BONK

Yes, folks, old 'Arry has come up with another world-shattering discovery.

Already well-known as the controversial tutor of Alexander, old 'Arry Aristotle today revealed his latest discovery to our reporter in Macedonia.

"Begonias don't bonk," says 'Arry. "And neither do nasturtiums!"

So sorry, lads and lasses, but you won't be getting any pollen on your pistils just yet!

Now if you were a worm, 'Arry says, he could do you a nice little spot of spontaneous generation: it seems they just close their eyes, think of Macedonia and whizz-bang-wallop, there you go, another few thousand little red wrigglers in the world. It makes you glad that you're not a flower or a worm, doesn't it, fellas?

Fourth in our exciting soul-searching series on the great faiths of the world.

Buddhism.

Just what is he up to?
Why is he so fat?
Is he trying to spontaneously generate?

All your questions answered on page 7.

Al, you're great!

37 not out!

Al smashes all-time record!

He must be pretty sure of the title now.

All-conquering 33-year-old Emperor Alexander has now gone 37 battles without defeat, shattering the old record as he scorches on to the title.

Those old championship rivals from Persia have really taken a beating, and Alex has even given Millwall fans something to dream about. He's hammered Issos, Tyre, Arbeles, Babylon, Susa and totally destroyed Persepolis, which has now been relegated to the second division.

The Big S says:
Nothing can stop him now.

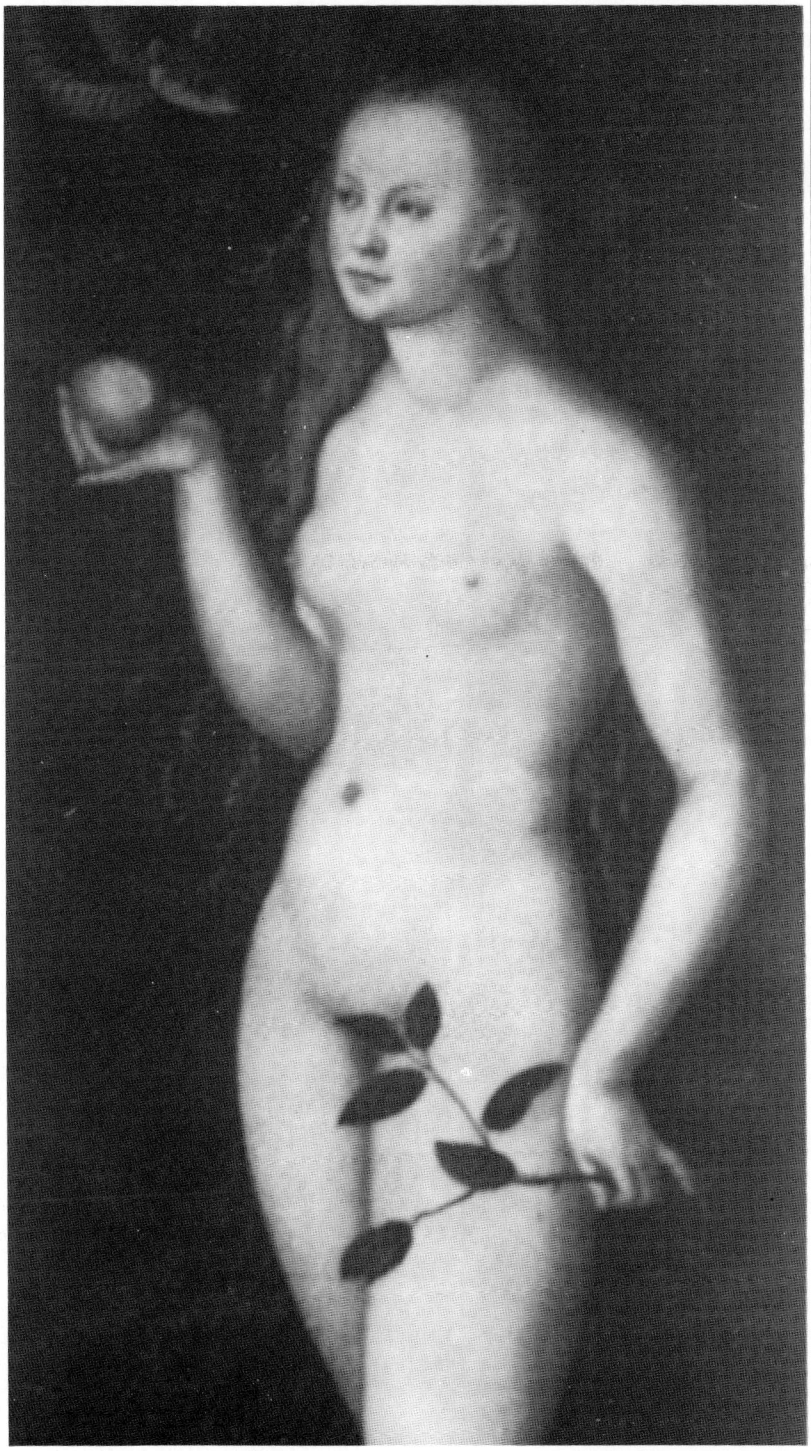

So begonias and nasturtiums don't do it! But we wouldn't mind if this little flower let her modesty drop and indulged in some not-quite-so spontaneous generation with us, would we, fellas?

GREAT SUPER FUN SPECIAL BIG S COMPETITION IN YOUR GREAT SUMMER FUN SUPER SPECIAL BIG S

25000 NOVELTY TOGA HANGERS TO BE WON!

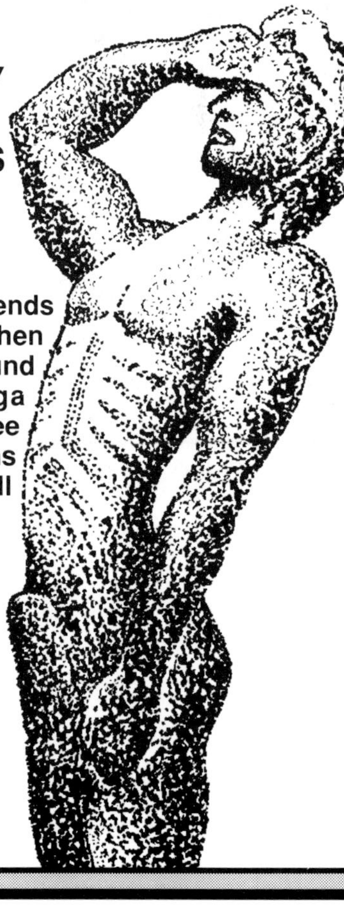

Give your friends a laugh when they pop round for a toga party, and see what happens when they all take their togas off!!!!!

Full details on page 9.

THE BIG S

MAGNUS S DIXIT: NOT-US ON YOUR NELLIBUS JULIUS! GO-US HOME-US ROME-US!

Date: Ides-of-March Eve | Price: One talent | Thought: Have a nice day!

VENI VIDI VICI

"It's disgusting! No way for a Roman Emperor to behave!" says Mark Anthony. "You wouldn't catch me dallying with an old slag like that!!!"

Read the lust-crazed, perverted story of Julius Caesar and Cleopatra, IN FULL DETAIL on pV

The tourist season got off to a great start yesterday when a whole load of Romans popped over the Channel.

But some of them seem to be crossing their bridges before they've started to build them!!!

When questioned by our reporter, **Mr Julius Caesar** said **"This looks a nice little place. I might as well conquer it now that I'm here."**

But a few hours later they were back on the boat with their bags of duty-free mead and woad.

"I'd almost forgotten," said Mr Caesar, "I've got to be at the Senate tomorrow. They'd kill me if I missed that!"

"But I'll be back," he shouted gaily as he went up the gangplank. "You'll see. I haven't conquered an island for ages."

ROMAN WEATHER FORECAST
HAIL, CAESAR!

Mrs Caesar having tea with friends

While the cat's away, they always say, and Mrs Caesar seems to have found a way of idling the years away while hubby conquers the known world.

When asked at Dover today about his wife's many and devoted admirers, Julius Caesar said they were all just good friends and that his wife was above suspicion.

The Big S says: Pull-us the other-us one-us!!!

YO HO HO YUS HUS HUS!

Big-us S-us Bing-us

Today's winning numbers

IX XIV XIX XXX XXXI LV LXIII LXXVII C CII

NOW WE'VE HEARD IT ALL: UP AND ATOM, LULU!

Loony Lucretius must have been hitting the love potions again!

Everything, so he says, is made up of little bits of things that go whizzing round and round and stick together to make other things which don't really exist, but are just lumps of these little things that go whizzing round and round for ever and ever.

The Big S says: Try leaving the amphora alone and go on the chariot, Lulu! Then things might not whizz round quite so fast.

BE A WINNER in our NEW BIG S super S-sational competition

MMDCLXIX SLAVES TO CRUCIFY!

Think of something really, really horrible to do to Spartacus . . . and the MMDCLXIX most original and most painful suggestions will win THEIR VERY OWN SLAVE TO CRUCIFY. **Entry forms on page XIII.**

SPORT: Pompey loses at home to Julius Caesar

THE BIG S

EVEN JULIUS CAESAR COULDN'T GET IT ENOUGH!!!

Date: A rather gaudy night. Price: There's beggary in the price that can be reckoned
Thought: What manner of thing **is** your crocodile?

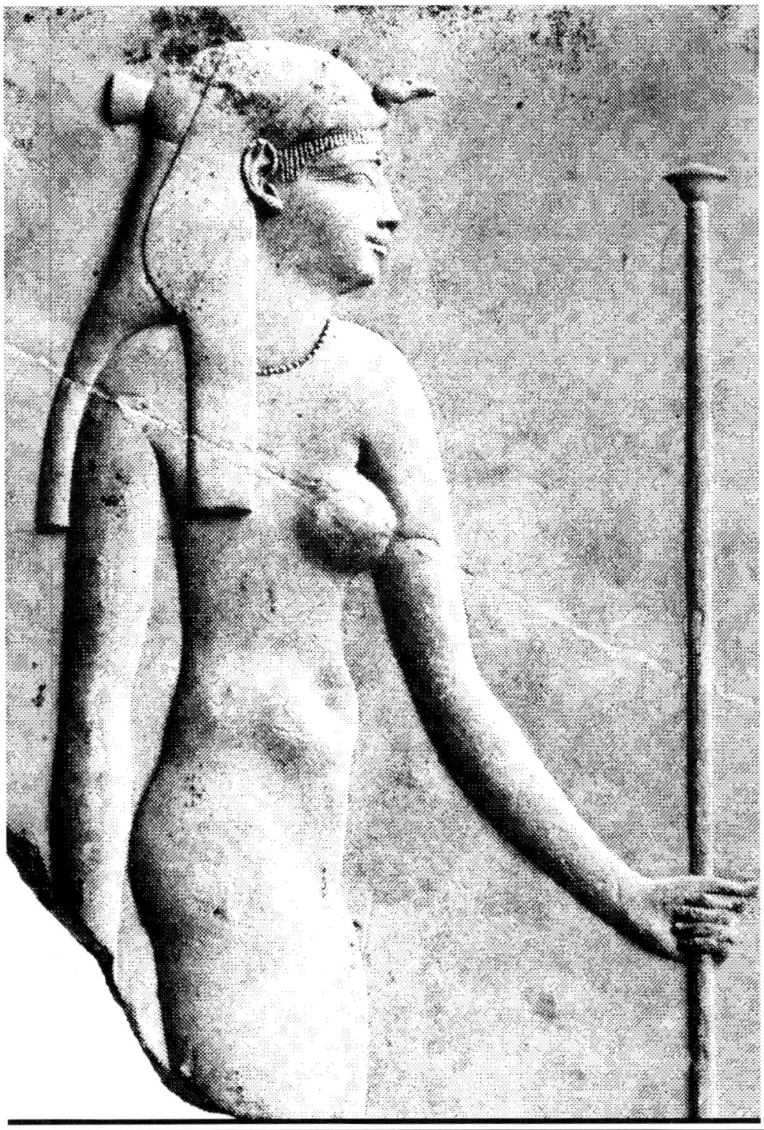

BUT NOW YOU CAN GET IT MORE OFTEN

Emperor decrees an extra day.

Yes, that is one thing that the lately demised ruler Julius Caesar did for the people, in between conquering the world and warming the bed for Antony down Egypt way.

With the new calendar we get an extra day every four years, and that **means an extra day of the Big S!**

And isn't that something to cheer about ?

SUPER SPECIAL BIG S SPORT

POMPEY LOSES AT HOME TO MARK ANTONY. DREADFUL SEASON CONTINUES. SEE FULL REPORT ON PAGE XII.

LET'S TO BILLIARDS!

Naughty-but-nice Naiad of the Nile Naomi just loves billiards and plays with her eunuchs every day!
Now she's looking for some stiffer competition, because the eunuchs aren't too good at ball games!
We say that if this little nymph needs a bit of extra practice, we could give her a bit extra to practise with any time she liked, couldn't we, fellas?

Perhaps all the NICE girls do love sailors, but there's a lot of VERY NAUGHTY GIRLS loving the soldiers here!!

Mad Mark Moons over ex-Monarch's Morsel

THE BIG S SAYS: A WORD OF ADVICE, ANTONY: DON'T PUSH IT TOO FAR!

AS THE POET SAID:

CAVEAT IMPER-ATOR

WHAT A PAIN IN THE ASP

BED DIDN'T GET COLD

That's what our reporter in Alexandria has to say as Mad Mark rushes back to Cleopatra. He may have been away for a great gap in time, but we're pretty certain the bed didn't get cold!!!

OUT FOR A ROW

Sultry 30-year-old Serpent-of-the-Nile Cleo was out for a row on the canal with a few friends when Mad Mark arrived back unexpectedly, having let the wide arch of the rang'd Empire fall.

And it didn't take long for a real steamy booze-and-sex session to get underway.

WE HAVE KISSED AWAY PINGDOMS

Even his battle-scarred companions are feeling the strain of feasting and drinking all night and off to a steaming bed-full of dusky delights as dawn peeps over the Pyramids.

THE BIG S

ROYAL SEX SCANDAL

John the Baptist loses head over Princess Salome, nymphet temptress of the Palace

Date: O. Something had better turn up soon. We've run out of numbers!
Price: Thirty pieces of silver. Thought: Mind your own business

DESERT RAT CUT DOWN TO SIZE

Handsome 60-year-old playboy King Herod was peeved when long-haired, unwashed, thirty-five-year-old, health-food-fanatic desert loony accused him of goings-on that were rather less than kosher!!!

John had taken time off from his job as attendant at a riverside bathing establishment to walk around, saying "Repent ye, ye that hump dead brother's wives!" Herod, who **has** been keeping it in the family a little, did not find that very amusing.

To cut a long story short, John will be wandering around a prison cell instead of the wilderness for a while now, and he'll be lucky to get even locusts and wild honey to eat.

SALOME MAKES VEILED COMMENTS

On a happier note, Herod told our reporter that he was looking forward to the little birthday celebration planned for that evening.

"Just a family affair," he said, "the wife and the kids and party tricks, the same as every year! I think little Salome might be planning something different, after her juggling went so sadly wrong last year. I don't know what she's up to, but she's been running round the Palace, taking down the net curtains and making all sorts of veiled comments. I suppose I shall see it all in the end."

WEATHERMEN BOOB AGAIN

- Storm causes havoc in city!
- Bank holiday crucifixions spoiled!

Why can't they ever get it right? They forecast a lovely bank holiday weekend, and the worst storm for years promptly arrives. In the city, people had their candles lit at midday, and it stayed pitch black until three. With all the taxes that the government spends on old men with corns and seaweed and goodness knows what other new-fangled technology, you'd think they'd have seen that one coming!!! It's the third Friday in a row now! For all the good they are, we might as well go back to the old methods where (cont page 5)

PASSOVER AMNESTY FARCE!

Come on, Pontius Pilate, enough is enough! What we want now is firm government, not free pardons to thieves, liars and murderers.

The Big S says

NAIL 'EM ALL UP

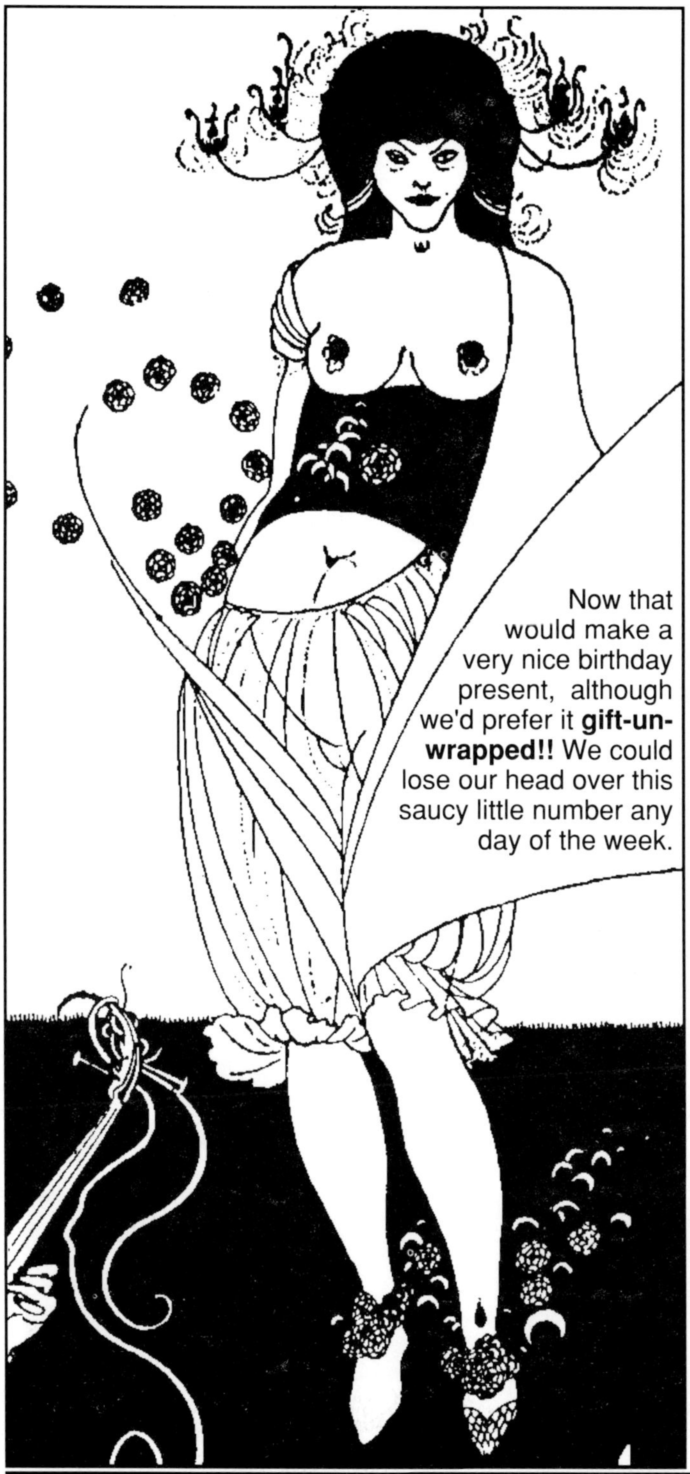

Now that would make a very nice birthday present, although we'd prefer it **gift-un-wrapped!!** We could lose our head over this saucy little number any day of the week.

THIS WEEK IN THE BIG S

POLL TAX SPECIAL

Confusion and fury as crowds hit the roads.

PLUS PLUS PLUS

Literary Big S-plement:

Ovid pens another little ditty.

There was a young lady from Rome,
Most partial to shaving foam,
She looks very swell-a,
Doesn't she, fella?
We wouldn't mind taking her home!

PLUS PLUS PLUS

Great Loonies of Our Time

WIFE-SWAPPING CULT SWINGS INTO TOWN.

"Love your neighbour" is the latest craze!

Now if we lived next door to Salome it might be interesting, but if you saw the old dragon who lives next door to me, you wouldn't be too keen.

PLUS PLUS PLUS

OVERCROWDING GETS WORSE

Tourist Board Boss slams Bethlehem hoteliers

THE BIG S

THE BIG S SAYS: JUST WHO ARE YOU CALLING ANCIENT?

Date: Just a little bit past A.D. Price: Annihilation Thought: All woads lead to Rome

IT'S THOSE ROMANS AGAIN

We've said it before, and we'll say it again:
GO-US HOME-US, ROME-US!!!

EXCLUSIVE SUPER FUN SUPER BIG S ANCIENT BRITISH LEISURE S-PLEMENT

CHARIOTEERING:

Boudicca road tests the latest models.

We don't know about the chariots, but Boudicca leaves us absolutely legless!

BEAUTY!

Ladies! Read the Big S Beauty tips!

-New fun things to do with woad!

-Keep your man interested with daring new designs

Yes, folks, they're back again! Slipped over on the late boat intent on conquering this sceptred isle. But we'll show them, won't we, lads?

SUPERIOR CIVILISATION, MY FOOT

We're not just going to sit round in our damp caves, gnawing at a bit of reindeer skin, with the kids crying because it's raining and they can't go out to play with the wolf, and the wife nagging, nagging, nagging, because the next-cave neighbours have just had fitted wall-to-wall gravel in their cave, while these Romans come over here and take over with their central-heating-this and central-heating-that and villas-this and villas-that and sex orgies with beautiful nubile slaves plucked from Araby's dusky shores, and marble bathrooms and baths and straight roads and orgies and fast, convertible chariots and fast, convertible slaves and bridges and money and orgies and mosaics and slaves and orgies and Vulgar Latin and Arches of Triumph and orgies and centurions and dirty pictures and tourists saying "Oh-us, Romulus, how-us quaint-us! Must-us be a native-us? Shall-us us-us draw-us his-us picture-us?" and orgies and laws and orgies and bricks and orgies and orgies and ablatives and datives and orgies and declensions (continued on pages II, III, IV, V, VI, VII, VIII, IX, X, XI, XII, XIII, XIV, XV, XVI, XVII, XVIII, XIX, XX, XXI, XXII, XXIII, XXIV, XXV and XXVI)

FASHION LATEST!

Two for the Ladies - Hims ancient and modern!

Our two true Brits will beat your dago poofter any day of the week, won't they, girls? He may look pretty with flowers in his hair and bows on his shoulders, but there's nothing like the sight of a good British warrior standing up and brandishing his equipment.

GREAT NORTH WALL APPEAL!

Neanderthal man re-discovered!

Help keep the hairy rabble out!

Keep our land fit for decent, honest law-abiding Ancient Britons!!!

The Big S says: Let's go down to Millwall and beat the (cont on page 2)

RULE, BRITANNIA, BRITANNIA RULES THE WAVES! BRITONS NEVER, EVER, EVER, WILL BE SLAVES!

THE BIG S

BIG S SPORT

Lions 623 Christians 0.

Home-town favourites make a meal of it.

Date: Beginning to decline   Price: III coins in a fountain   Thought: When in Rome, ...

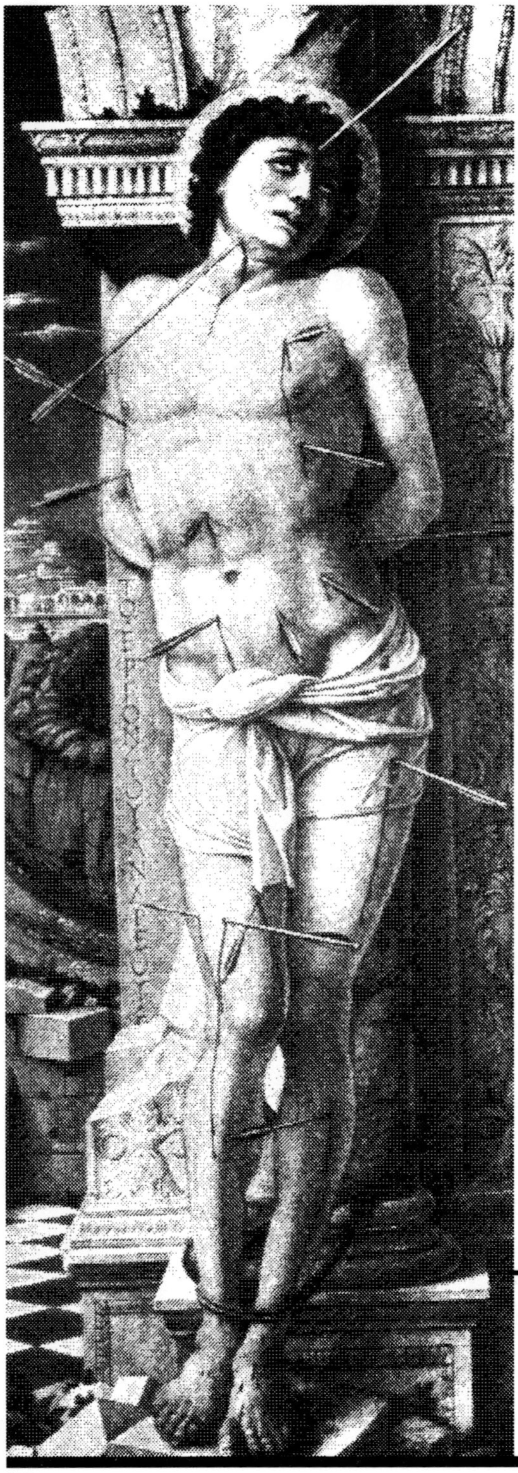

BIG S IN-DEPTH INQUIRY: ARE WE GOING SOFT?

The Big S says this easy living is making us soft.

FACT: Last week **four** of the injured **gladiators** were **not** finished off in the arena!!!

FACT: Some so-called **sporting authorities** have called for a **limit** to the amount of lead to be permitted in **boxers'** gloves!!!

FACT: Many of the city's 32000 prostitutes are going weeks without being beaten and raped!

FACT: Some are calling for **crucifixion** to be brought back!
And **who would pay** for the wood?
The **taxpayer!**
And who would pay for the labour to make the crosses?
And the disposal of any remains?
The taxpayer!
It's not the criminals and the Christians who are going to pay, is it?
It's you and me!
AND WE'D HAVE TO FEED THE LIONS!!!
These softies are killing sport!

The Big S says: What's the use of Nero setting a good example, if we don't follow it? Throw the wets to the lions before it's too late.

NUMBER FIVE IN OUR SUPER S-CITING S-CLUSIVE SERIES

GREAT FAITHS OF THE WORLD

CHRISTIANITY

Why are they such party-poopers?
Why do they like to fight lions?

Our reporter managed to interview leading Christians just before they were all executed!!!

Read about this crazy new fad on page 15

ONE HUNDRED AND EIGHTY!

This year's easy winner in the Christian World Darts Championship with a perfect set of arrows.

NICE ONE NERO

Popular playboy Emperor Nero last night delighted the court with a dazzling performance on the fiddle.

The highlight of the evening was his rendering of the Fireworks Music, made even more impressive by the flickering lights of one or two hovels burning in the more common parts of town.

It has been rumoured that the display got a little out of hand, but the plebs would have begged to be given the honour of burning their houses themselves, if they had known just how much pleasure it would give their beloved Emperor.

The army has arrested a few thousand Christians who will soon confess to setting fire to the city in an attempt to embarrass our glorious Emperor.

We needn't tell you that Nero was not amused, and has ordered an inquiry. As a precautionary measure, and pending the results of the inquiry, all Christians have been executed.

After the Emperor's performance, millionaire playboy and imperial advisor Seneca did suggest that the Emperor's fingering could have been a little better in one or two of the pizzicatos. The Emperor, with that flashing wit which has so endeared him to his loyal subjects, turned and said, "Take a powder, Senna Pod!" Of course, being a loyal and loving subject himself, Seneca rushed off to gratify his dear Emperor's wish.

The funeral is set for XIV hours this afternoon.

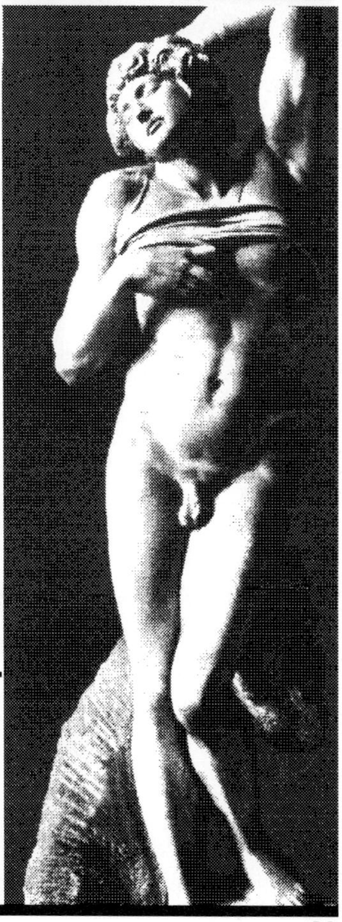

Big S S-clusive Time-Share Opportunity!

Readers are offered the exclusive chance to snap up time-share opportunities in the new centre of Imperial Chariot-setting Patricians.

Basking by a beach of golden sand, the new resort of POMPEII has got it ALL for all the family.

Shopping centres, luxury villas, surfaced roads, super brothels: everything you need for the ideal country-and-beach-get-away-from-the-office-and-the-stink-of-the-traffic-and-the-boring-regular-neighbourhood-orgy-with-the-same-old-slaves-and-same-old-perversions weekend and holiday break.

Easy charioting from Rome and Naples.

DON'T STAY IN ROME AND RISK HAVING YOUR HOUSE BURNED DOWN BY CHRISTIANS!!! MOVE OUT TO POMPEII NOW!!!

And here's another very nice one! We're all dying to be his little slaves. Nero may like fiddling while Rome burns, but when I felt like a spot of fiddling myself, I could certainly play an air on his little G-string, couldn't you, fellas?

THE BIG S

Date: It's gone too dark to see
Price: One candle
Thought: I think we're going to regret this one, Vortigern.

Filthy Barbarian Hordes Invasion Special

THE ENGLISH ARE COMING

BIG S EXCLUSIVE INTERVIEW

"It just ain't good enough!!!" say the cavewives of Penge.

Yes, the cavewives of Penge were angry this morning after the latest wave of Barbarian invaders had surged through!
"You just get over one lot," an old woman of 17 told us, "you just get over one lot of raping and pillaging and looting and murdering, you just get the cave back nice and tidy, and the next lot arrive. And it's up with your loincloth and over on your back on the best floral-covered boulder again!!!"

The Prime Minister in Wales at the Druids' Conference.

RULE BRITANNIA, BRITANNIA RULES THE WAVES, BRITONS NEVER, EVER, EVER, EVER, EVER, EVER WILL BE SLAVES

DAMN VANDALS!

THERE'S NOT A PHONEBOX IN EUROPE STILL WORKING!

SEE SPECIAL REPORT ON PAGE 8.

ELECTION SPECIAL

Attila the Hun to stand in Millwall by-election? Neanderthal party picks up points.

SAVAGE LUSTS

"I'm right sick and tired of assuaging their savage lusts," she continued.

"Yea," another went on, "and if it ain't the Goths, it's the Visigoths, and if it ain't the Visigoths, it's the Ostrogoths. I'd just like to know what the government is going to do about it!"

QUESTIONS ASKED

And that is what men and women up and down the country would like to know.

Why have the entire government decided to hop it down to Wales?

Are they really going to the International Druids' Conference?

Or have they just done a bunk?

WE DEMAND AN ANSWER!!!

The Big S says: Come on, King Vortigern, play fair. You invited these English savages over here in the first place.

And we're sick of hearing the old reply that you didn't know they were going to bring the wife and kids and settle in.

We want to know what you're going to do about it!

Because the way you're going now, these primitive animals might be here for ever.

We are not too sure about Hengist and Horsa and all these filthy hordes, but we do know that this little Barbarian Miss has got lots of SAXon appeal, no matter what ANGLE you look from.

THE BIG S

ROYAL SEX SCANDAL

Date: I think we're going backwards
Price: A sprig of mistletoe
Thought: She hath proved herself a lover of good knights

KNIGHT LAYS HER MAJESTY: GUILTY OF LESE-MAJESTE

Fairies in forest!

The Big S says: This has gone far enough.
We say the Knights of the Round Table should not go round doing things with fairies in the forest where INNOCENT CHILDREN might be having a picnic!!! While we do not approve of the familiarity of Sir Lancelot with the Queen, at least **he** is not a raving poofter, or a pinko, or a
(continued on page 3)

Visit the
Great Ideal Castle Exhibition!
See this year's super exciting new range of round tables

Property news

Hovel prices boom as invading Saxons buy up everything.
The Big S says: Go home, English, and take your football team with you!

This Sir Galahad is very prompt to offer his assistance when he finds little scorchers like this in a state of undress.
We'd lend any damsel in distress our weapon, wouldn't we, fellas? but we can't promise it would be that big.

CAUGHT AT COURT AT CAMELOT

OH LA LA LANCELOT!

Naughty knight in naughty night in a right royal bedchamber

It had to happen one day, for the goings-on have been going on for far too long.
Yes, folks, this time Sir Lancelot has really been caught with his scutum down! He has well and truly sullied his escutcheon!

No sooner had King Arthur gone out hunting one bright, moonlit night, than another knight went out after quite some other game.
But where the King **left** Queen Guinevere's bed to hunt, Oh-La-La-Lancelot **got into** her bed to do **his** hunting.

QUEEN TO GET A RIGHT ROYAL ROASTING!!!

King Arthur was not amused when he got home to find a pile of bodies in the bedroom, his queen undone, and the dirty rascal fled to the Castle of the

(continued on page 7)

Queen risks all for one knight of passion!

SUPER BIG S SPORT: FOOTBALL

Llanfairpwllgwyngyllgogerychwyrndrobwllllantisiliogogogoch City 9 England 0

"This was an encouraging result," says the new England manager. "My boys played well under difficult conditions and against a good team."
"Yes," he added, "a most encouraging result."

"Give us another few centuries," he claimed, "and my boys will be able to beat any team on Anglesey, or the Isle of Wight! And then the sky's the limit: who knows, perhaps one day, with a bit of luck, we'll even beat Egypt or the Cameroons!!!"

The Big S says: WHO? Knock it off! We've heard it all before, and we'll hear it all again. You'll never learn to play so why bother spouting all this bull-

(continued on page 5)

THE BIG S

Holy Roman Emperor, my foot!!!

Big Charlie goes too far!

Date: 800 a.d. Price: Your honour Thought: Big feet never prosper.

POO! WHAT A PONK!

CAROLUS MAGNUS CAROLUS MAGNUS EST!

or, as they say round here, Charles the Big is a big Charlie!

Queen Mum Bertha was always known for big feet, but son Charlie has been putting his in it recently, and causing a bit of a stink.

Now he's nipped off to Rome to be crowned Holy Roman Emperor by Pope Leo the Louse.

Now old Leo wouldn't recognise something holy even if it jumped out and bit him.

Our reporter tells us that Leo was recently kicked out of his job for quite unholy practices.

Now he has worked a good one on Charlie, promising to make him Emperor if he, Charlie, helps him get his job back.

And Charlie the Big fell for it like the right Big One that he is!

Charles is desperately trying to outdo his Granddad who hammered the Moors a few years ago down at Poitiers.

The Big S says: he just hasn't got it in him.

Roncesvalles was a disaster.

It's one thing having an oliphant, but it's another thing knowing how and when to use it!

BIG S LITERARY BIG S-PLEMENT

Tempting tale-teller from the east Scheherazade keeps the Sultan up for 1001 nights.

This year's sizzling bestseller, that Arabian blockbuster, The 1001 Nights, has just hit the scroll-stores over here.

And what a sizzler it is!!!

It's got more sultanas than a fruit cake!

All the favourites are in there: Sinbad, Aladdin, Ali Baba, although why those Pagan Persians are so interested in Christmas pantomime stories is a mystery to us.

But it's a rattling good read, full of passion and romance and the dusky maidens of Araby and su-

(continued on page 5)

Our second scroll for review this week is Beowulf.

Beowulf is a home-grown product. It's a grisly tale of monsters and a nouveau riche parvenu.

We have never been overly partial to heroic epics, and we find the single alliterative line and the one-upmanship of its allusions both tedious and monotonous. Monsters and dragons and slaying is all right in its place, but the story would have been much richer, more complete with a touch of romance, some warmth and human affection, tenderness or at least a bit of

(continued on page 3)

Great faiths of the World. Sixth in our exciting series:

Islam

Is six times a day too much?
Could your man manage it?
How come they get carpets to kneel on?

These and other searching questions about this latest fashion in Gods answered on page 8!!!

It's not hard to see how the Sultan managed it, is it, fellas? I'm sure we could stay up for a pretty long time if she would come and tell us a bed-time story!

New crackdown on law and order

4500 Saxon demonstrators were beheaded yesterday when they came out of their hovels to complain about all the looting and raping and pillaging the Army has been doing as part of Charlie the Big's new pacification policy. Charlie has decided to honour the Saxons by including them in his Empire and by extending to them the peace and security and all the other benefits that come with belonging to a large Empire.

"However, I am determined," said Charlie, "to create order and justice throughout my lands, so that decent, honest, law-abiding subjects can go about their daily business without fear. There has been too much civil unrest recently."

The Big S says: Good old Charlie. That's what we call re-habilitation. They won't demonstrate again in a hurry.

BIG S SPORT:

Charlemagne 4500 Saxons 0. Charlie wins by a head!

THE BIG S

Date:1060 Price: A pair of scissors Thought: If only the Dark Ages had ended! I didn't see a thing

MIDDLESBOROUGH RAIDED AGAIN!!!

"Worse than when Millwall played here in the semi-final," one Middlesborough resident told our reporter today after the horrific looting and raping and pillaging and killing that had gone on during the recent Viking raid.

This is the eightieth time that the Vikings have raided Middlesborough and the locals have had enough!

Just what is Harold doing about it? That is the question on everybody's lips up here.

The Big S says: We can't answer for Harold, but our advice is to just ignore them and they'll go away. Besides, you can't be too angry with anybody daft enough to raid Middlesborough, can you?

P*SS*D AS A CANUTE

The Royal Wedding celebrations came to an unexpected but memorable climax last night.

ROYAL WEE

King Canute was in a jovial mood, having quaffed a considerable amount of ale, when he suddenly rose to his feet, looked blindly around him and shouted, "My goodness, I could do with a Royal Wee!"

KING GOES FOR A PADDLE

He staggered out of the Royal Tent, mistook his direction and was last seen, a memorable, poignant vision of true royalty that will haunt the memory of those privileged to be present, laughing, puking, water lapping round his royal orb and sceptre, shouting in his quaint Danish accent, "Get back, you filthy Ba-

continued on page five

Perhaps Old Canute was not that daft after all! We'd be happy to do a spot of paddling with this little bathing beauty any time at all.

FREE INSIDE BIG S LEISURE S-PLEMENT

HOLIDAYS

Big S-clusive offer

Can you believe it's already time to think of holidays again? Well it is! and we are offering a

Super Big S Fun-filled Trip to Jerusalem.

See the sights!
Slay the Saracens!
The group will be led by the Bishop of Bamberg!

- **FREE travel bag!!!**
- **FREE chastity belt to all leaving wife behind!!!**
- **FREE super quality Red Cross T shirt!!!**

See page 7 for details.

COOKERY

Cook, cook, cookability! Exclusive offer: Alfred's great recipe for cakes!

GRACIOUS LIVING

How to be the perfect hostess First in a great new series by Lady Macbeth from her bonny wee castle in Scotland.

ROYAL SEX SCANDAL

READY, WILLING AND ABLE!!!

Ethelred may have been Unready, but his wife isn't!

The King is dead, Long live the King is the motto going around the royal bedchamber this week. No sooner is hubby Ethelred safely tucked away underground, than saucy consort Emma is safely tucked away in Canute's bed.

A right royal case of Off with the Old and On with the New!

GO GO GO LADY GO!

The Big S says: this will bring the crowds back to city centres after closing hours.

BAREBACK RIDING WITH A SADDLE!

Lovely Lady Godiva did a bit of bare-back riding through the streets of Coventry yesterday, but it wasn't the horse's back that was bare!

Bold new initiative launched by Earl Leofric.

The luscious wife of this local noble went in for a spot of personal asset-stripping before going for a quick canter round the block.

"It is not just a cheap gimmick, or some kinky thrill," dribbled loony Leo the Lewd to our reporter, "it is a serious commercial effort to combat the spread of out-of-town trading hovels, and to reduce the taxes paid by each individual by enlarging the number of taxable subjects. It is better to have 1000 churls paying 1 penny than 50 petty bourgeois paying 10 pennies. Simple economics. You wait, it will catch on sooner or later! And the nudity is completely justified. It is a necessary and integral part of the presentation. Anyway, what's so wrong with kinky thrills? My wife and I often

(continued on page 7)

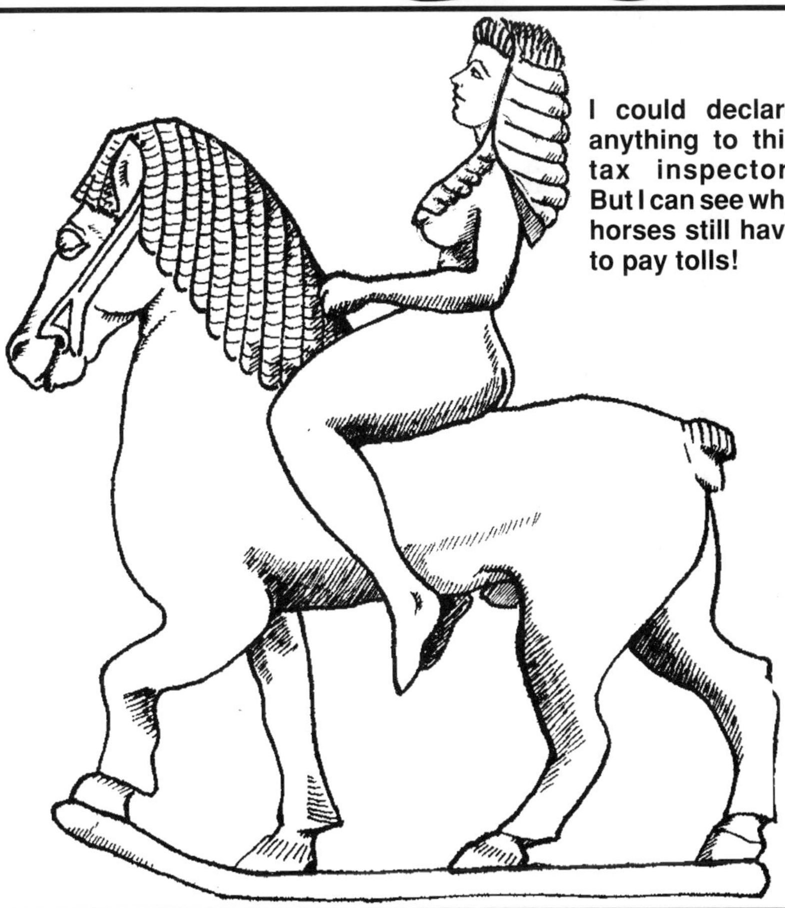

KINKY EARL SENDS WIFE ON PEEP-SHOW RIDE

PEEPING TOM GETS HIS EYEFUL!!!

The lovely, lissome, long-haired lassy provided even more excitement when she pulled her clothes off than when the local football team pulled off the impossible and won the cup.

But Lady Go was not pulling any more off and she kept her locks firmly around her as she cantered around, making more than one randy citizen long for the day when the Eton crop would

(continued page 3)

THE BIG S

As we say over here HOP IT, FROGGIES or si vous preferez

Date: 1066 Price: Un franc Thought: More Hastings, less speedings

ALLEZ A LA MAISON GUILLAUME

You can't just come over here and conquer us.

This is a country with hundreds of years of traditions, stable government, a much-loved monarchy and time-hallowed institutions!!!!

No snail-eating, garlic-reeking, limp-wristed Vikingo-Normano-Franco poofters are going to come over and push us English around, are they, lads?

HAROLD GETS AN EYEFUL!!!

Bad luck, Harold. Isn't it always the way?

Yes, folks, that's the way it goes! One minute you're up, next minute you're down!
The latest lucky winner in our exciting Big S competitions, poor King Harold, had just taken delivery of his BIG S -exclusive-Peeping-Tom periscope and had nipped down to the coast for a glimpse of some saucy French bathing beauties who had popped over for a day on the sands.

And, my goodness, there were some real corkers!
Well, they always say you shouldn't look up when the birds are going past, but Harold did!

MORE THAN SAND CASTLES

And there was this bunch of Normans who had also nipped over the Channel and who were planning on building more than sand-castles!
This was no mere shopping trip to stock up on woollies for the winter! Things started to turn a little unpleasant, the way they do when there are boys together on a beach, with a bit of pushing and shoving and then old Harold looked up and this Norman,
(continued on page 3)

FRENCH TO BE MADE COMPULSORY IN SCHOOLS

Willie the Conk, a true Bastard if ever we came across one, is certainly not going about winning friends and influencing people with his new ideas.
First it was a big book with a list of everything he owns! What that means is a big book with everything **we** own and that **he** plans to take from us. He'll be saying water belongs to him next!!!
Megalomania, we call that.
Go and lie down in a dark dungeon, Willie, and hope it goes away!

AND NOW IT'S FRENCH FOR EVERYBODY!

Well, we'll tell you right now that we ain't going to parler no francais for you nor nobody else. We're not going to abandon the language of Shakespeare for no jumped-up Froggie poofter!
Mettez cela dans votre pipe et fumez le, grande tete!
You needn't think that just because you have an enormous army, are ruthlessly cruel, obstinate and determined and are willing to viciously crush anybody who stands in your way ...er... er..
Le Grand S dit: Vive le francais! Vivent les Normans!

So this is what those saucy mademoiselles are wearing at the sea-side this year.
Vive la France!

Litteraire Grand S-plement
Special hit-parade.
Number Un Best-seller:
Le Rubaiyat d'Omar Khayyam.
- - - Grand poete et mathematicien persian ecrit poemes exotiques.
- - - Quatrains epigrammatiques revealent cynicisme et pessimisme.
Seeez les details full sur page 7

BIG S SUPER S-PECIAL PRIZE FOR THE BEST IDEA ON HOW TO THANK OUR LOVELY NORMAN CONQUERORS FOR COMING OVER HERE TO DO ALL THEIR LOVELY RAPING AND LOOTING AND PILLAGING AND KILLING!!!

Send your ideas in a French letter as soon as possible.

P.S. Will the loony-tune who keeps sending us bits of embroidery please stop it? It's a stupid idea and would never work.

THE BIG S

Date:1189 Price: Jerusalem Thought: Absence makes the heart grow fonder

What a good boy!

Philip-Augustus went and sat on the throne before setting off for Jerusalem.
The Big S says: We thought Froggies only had a hole in the ground!!!

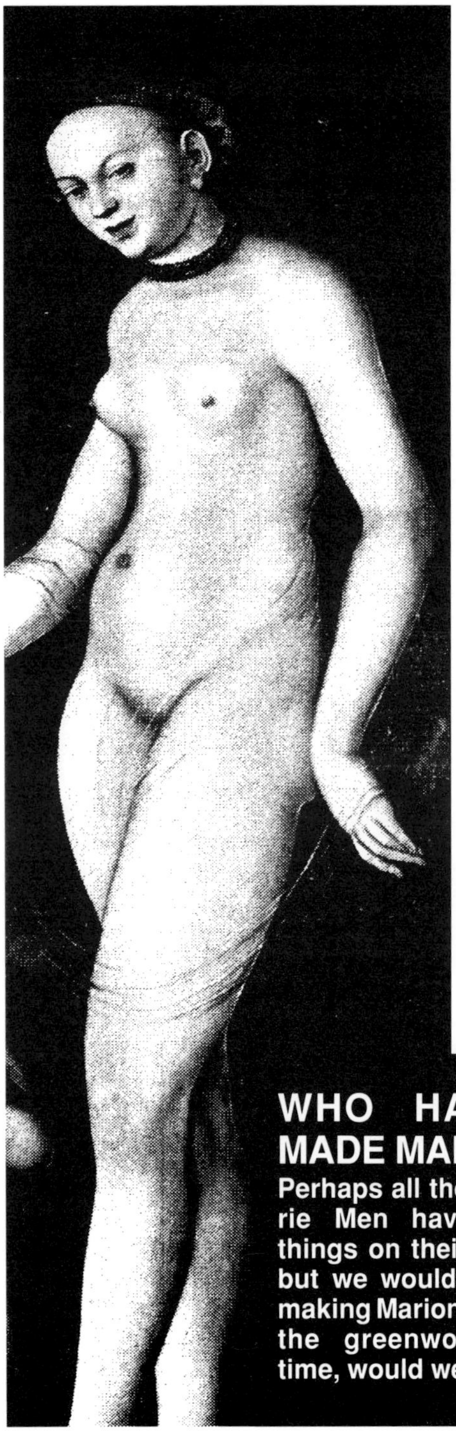

BIG S SUPER SPECIAL EXCLUSIVE INTERVIEW

Our reporter caught up with ROBIN HOOD yesterday as the notorious outlaw was once again fleeing the Sheriff after another deed of derring-do at a sub-post office.

PRE-ELECTION GALLOP POLL

As they galloped desperately through the forest, Mr Hood gave his exclusive opinions about the forthcoming election battle.

Reporter: Now then, Robin. Is it true that Maid Marion has got enormous ... No, I'm sorry, wrong bit of parchment. I'll start again. Now then, Rob, what do you reckon to these election thingies? Who are you and all your Merrie Men going to vote for? The Downtrodden Masses Party or the Screw-you-United-Conser....
Watch out! You let that branch swing back straight in my face.

Robin: Sorry! Neither party will make much difference to my business. I shall carry on with my own personal plan of social action and wealth re-distribution.

Reporter: But if you carry on robbing the rich and giving to the poor, then soon the rich are going to be poorer than the poor who will have become rich. Then you are going to have to rob the poor to give to the rich. So why bother? If you want to rob the poor, and I mean really rob them, comprehensively, mercilessly, if you want a thorough-going, soul-searching, teeth-grinding fleecing of the general populace, and and if you want to to save yourself a whole lot of trouble into the bargain, leave it to the professionals, **let the Government do it for you: vote Screw-You-United-Conserv...**

(continued page 5)

WHO HASN'T MADE MARION?

Perhaps all those Merrie Men have other things on their minds, but we wouldn't mind making Marion down in the greenwood any time, would we, fellas?

PLAN TO MAKE SAINT OF THE MURDERER'S MATE

Twenty years after twisted archbishop Thomas à Becket insisted that a priest convicted of murder should be merely sacked, his sick friends are talking of making him a saint!
Now one of the best things to happen for a long time was when old Tom kicked the bucket, so let's hope the boys who sorted him out are still around to polish off his perverted pals.

The Big S says: Good riddance to bad rubbish.

Rich the Itch is off again

ANTS IN THE ROYAL PANTS

We don't know about a Lion's heart, but he's certainly got very itchy feet.

This time King Richard is off on a nice little cruise round the Med and then down to Jerusalem for a bit of fun with the Saracens.

Very nice if you can get it, I'm sure.

The crown has hardly had time to settle on his head, and his poor old Dad is still warm in his grave, and he's off gallivanting instead of re-conquering all the bits the Froggies have stolen from us recently, and teaching them a lesson. And what's worse, **he's going on holiday with them.** It's the same super brat-pack as ever: Rich the Itch, Fred the Red, so-called Holy Roman Emperor and hairy layabout from Germany who's already done for Italy more than the whole Millwall fan club could do on a good day, and Phil the Conk from gay Paree who has done for friendship what Attila the Hun did for East-West relations.

You almost feel sorry for the Saracens sometimes.

THE BIG S SAYS: WHAT ABOUT ALL THE JOBS AT HOME, DICK?

THE BIG S

CHINA DEVASTATED BY VISITING TARTARS

MILLWALL MANAGER ASKS FOR THE VIDEO

Date: 1220 Price: One crown Thought: I'm beginning to see the light.

WHAT A SAUCE

—Tartar chief Genghis Khan is moving over here!—

Old Genghis has been putting himself about a bit off in the wilds of Asia for quite some time now. First it was Mongolia, and then he started going around conquering China and India and other unimportant little places over there.

BUT NOW HE'S MOVING WEST!!

Now that's quite enough, Genghis. You can turn the Gobi into a desert if you like, but we don't want you over here, devastating and looting and raping and pillaging. We can do that ourselves, thank you very much.

The Big S says: Taa-taa, Genghis, you khan go back home now!

HE TALKS TO THE BIRDS, THAT'S WHY THEY PUT HIM AWAY!

Those old eye-ties are at it again. Rich playboy Francis of Assisi has gone clear round the bend, giving away his money and talking to the little birdies -and this time it's the feathered ones, not the kind he's been chasing up till now.

FAMILY CONCERN

His family is so concerned -especially about the money, so some gossips have suggested- that they have sent him to a private clinic in Assisi to get him dried-out.

See full story on page 11.

LOTS OF PAPER BUT NO LAND!

Phew! Feudalism is a bore!

Barons are revolting. Feudalism threatened. First step taken towards a written constitution!

King John has never had much land, and now he hasn't got much of anything else either.

Knocked for 6 by brother Richard's ex-crusading companion, Phil of France, and thrashed by Roman Pope and inventor of the horseless carriage, Innocenti, he's now been turned into mincemeat by the Barons.

No longer will the King be able to go around doing whatever he likes, imposing taxes or military service whenever he feels like it.

THE BARONS ARE GOING TO DO IT INSTEAD!

This means a whole new era of unprecedented peace and prosperity under the benevolent guidance of the Barons!

The Big S says: Good riddance to bad rubbish!

LITERARY BIG S-PLEMENT

"JESUS, MOSES AND MOHAMMED: THE THREE GREAT IMPOSTORS."

Scientist, scholar and Holy Roman Emperor Fred II causes stir with new book!

The Big S says he's gone too far and must be stopped!

It's a dangerous example and must be stopped. Kings aren't brainy! What happened to good old traditional royal qualities of looting and pillaging and killing and raping and sitting on the throne holding your orb?

The Big S says: Knock it off, Fred, before any other king starts imagining he's got brains!

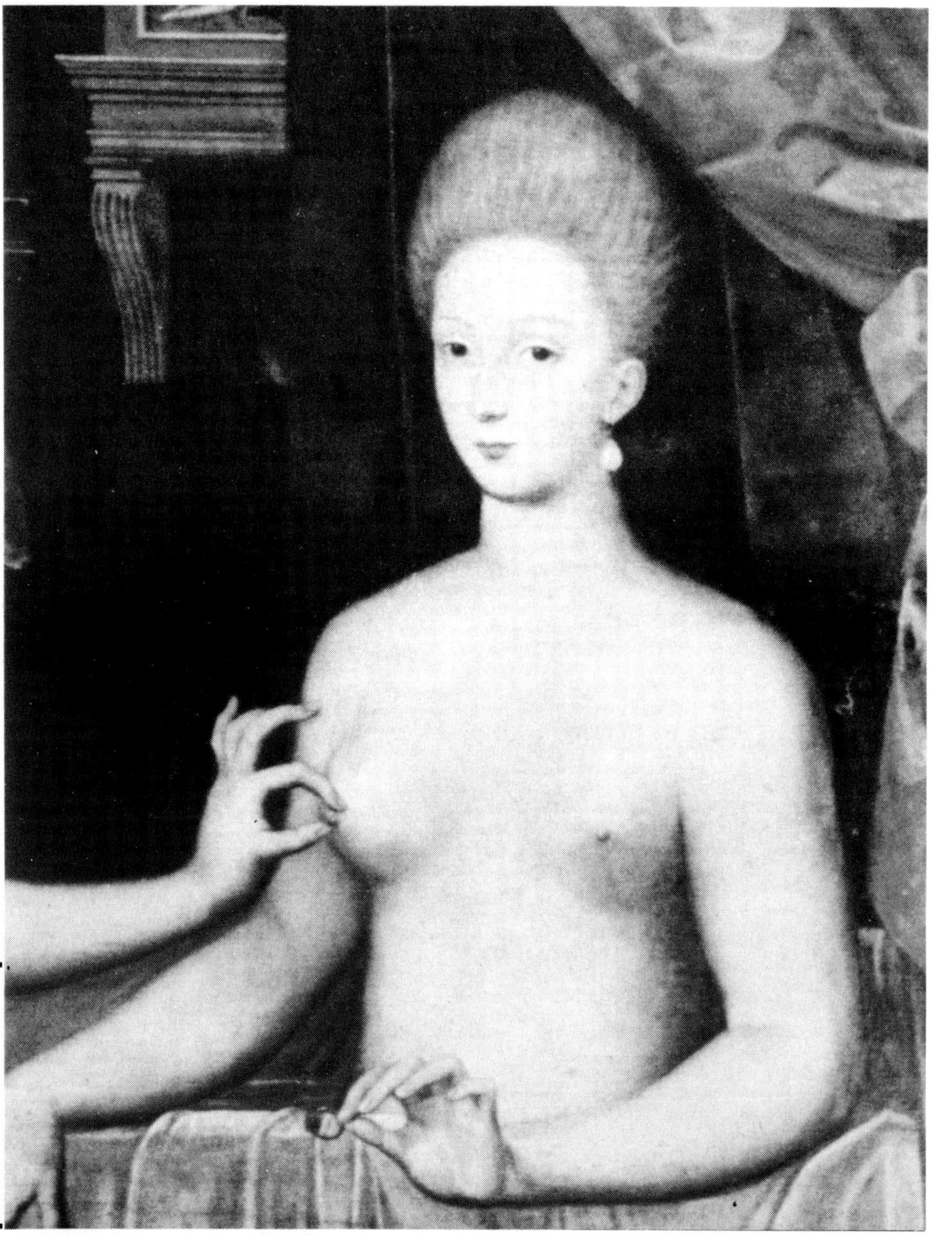

EXCUSE FINGERS!

If this is what they mean by an oath of FEEL-TY, then we'd be prepared to swear on this little cutie, wouldn't we, fellas?

THE BIG S

PLEASURE DOMES IN XANADU

Big S S-clusive story
Marco Polo at the court of Kublai Khan!!!

WITH PICTURES!!!
SEE PAGE 7

Date: 1283 Price: One dead daffodil Thought: A time to be born, a time to die, Dai.

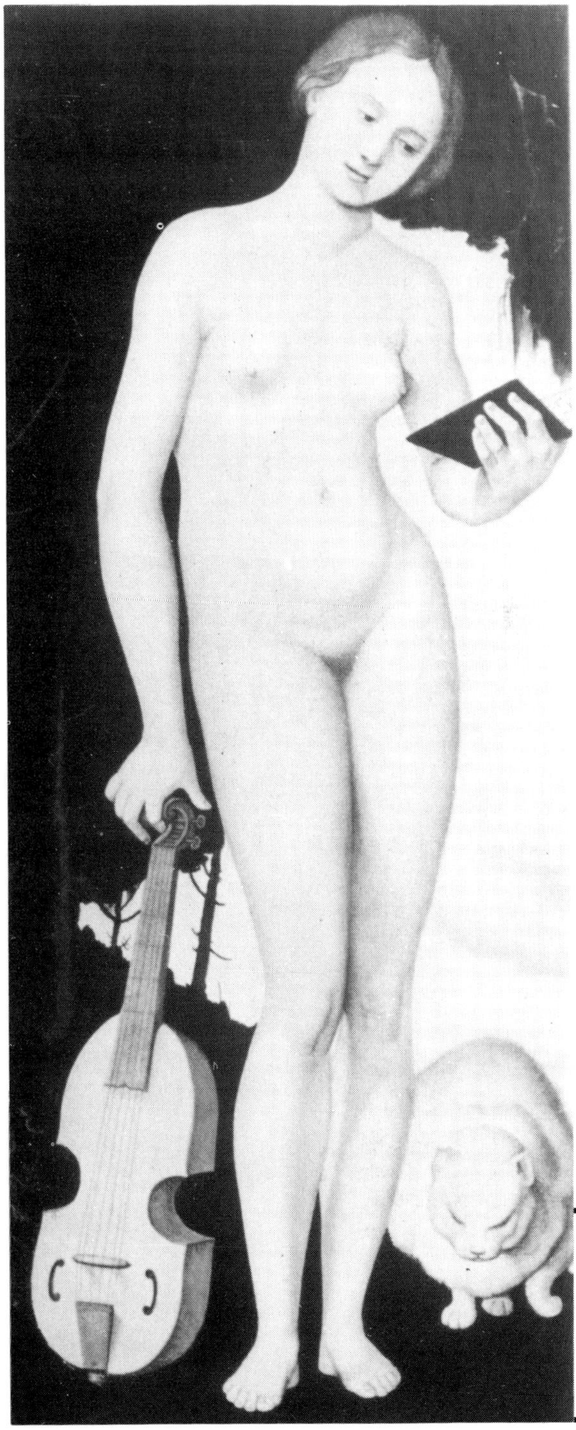

EYE-TIE POOFTERS GET THE VOTE!!!

No wonder they call the place Florence!

Just the right name for the bunch of limp-wristed, pasta-sucking poofters that live there!

Now they've adopted something called a written constitution! They elect a council to rule the city for the benefit of the inhabitants!!! What a bunch of ninnies! Did you ever hear of anything so soft?

And would you believe there's a fellow living there, a Mr Dante, who earns his living writing fairy-stories?

And a Mr Cimabue who gets paid for painting pictures?

And we've heard rumours that a certain Mr Jotto is jotting down pictures of ... guess-who? Yes, that's right, loony-tune Francis who talked to the little dickie birds.

The Big S says it'll never come to anything. There's nothing like a good disembowelling to make a man!

GREAT LOONIES OF OUR TIME

ROGER BACON

The Big S says Go home, Roger, your bacon's cooked.

They say you can't make a silk purse out of a sow's ear, but you can certainly get some rashers out of a side of bacon.
And Roger Bacon will be making some more of his rash statements every day all this week in our new

SUPER BIG S SUPER FUN SCIENCE BIG S-PLEMENT!
Read all about his flying machines and horseless carriages.
Find out his 1001 fun things to do with your girlfriend and his latest brainwave, the microscope.
Carry out your own experiments on the relative speeds of light and sound.

Yes, it's all in this week's SUPER BIG S SUPER SCIENCE FUN SPECIAL BIG S-PLEMENT.
See page 9.

They say that music is the food of love, and we'd be happy to indulge in a spot of pizzicato with this little number. We'd even come back for seconds, wouldn't we, Oliver?

GOTCHA TAFFIE

If you can keep your head -and your bowels- when all about you are losing theirs, then you're not a Taffie!!!

Barbaric Welsh terrorist leader, "Prince" Taffie, brother of ex-"prince" Lou the Two, executed last year, was sentenced yesterday in Shrewsbury in a real carnival atmosphere.

The judge really got into the spirit of the occasion, providing a really good day-out and a super spectacle by having Dai boy dragged through the streets tied to horses' tails first, and then by having him disembowelled !

LAUGH? MEDICAL ATTENTION NEEDED

You should have seen Dai's face! Talk about laugh? Some people in the crowd almost died laughing and needed medical assistance!

The actual hanging was something of an anti-climax after that, but the festive atmosphere was soon re-captured when he was drawn and quartered.

SUPER BIG-S FUN

A new super-Big-S-Fun innovation was the competition for the pieces afterwards!

This attracted a top-class field of contestants and there was a marvellous struggle between teams representing the North and the South of England for the right shoulder quarter.

At one moment, competition did get a little too keen, but order and harmony and the nice family atmosphere was restored when each of the competing teams was awarded a quarter of the "Prince" each.

The head will go to London, where readers will be able to see it, in a matching pair with that of his brother Lou the Two, in a **super new Big S show-stopping special opening at the Tower next Wednesday.**

The Big S says get there early to avoid disappointment.

Indeed to goodness, there's a lazy lot they are, isn't it?
These three Taffs have been hanging around here for ages. They're probably waiting for the tavern to open, like the rest of their disgusting race.
You'd think they'd be grateful for being conquered, so that we can civilise them a bit!

THE BIG S

LIFE IN THE CITY
Super Special S-clusive Report on the Jungle that is London

Date: 1310 Price: Not another apple core! Thought: We don't like fruits!

DID YOU

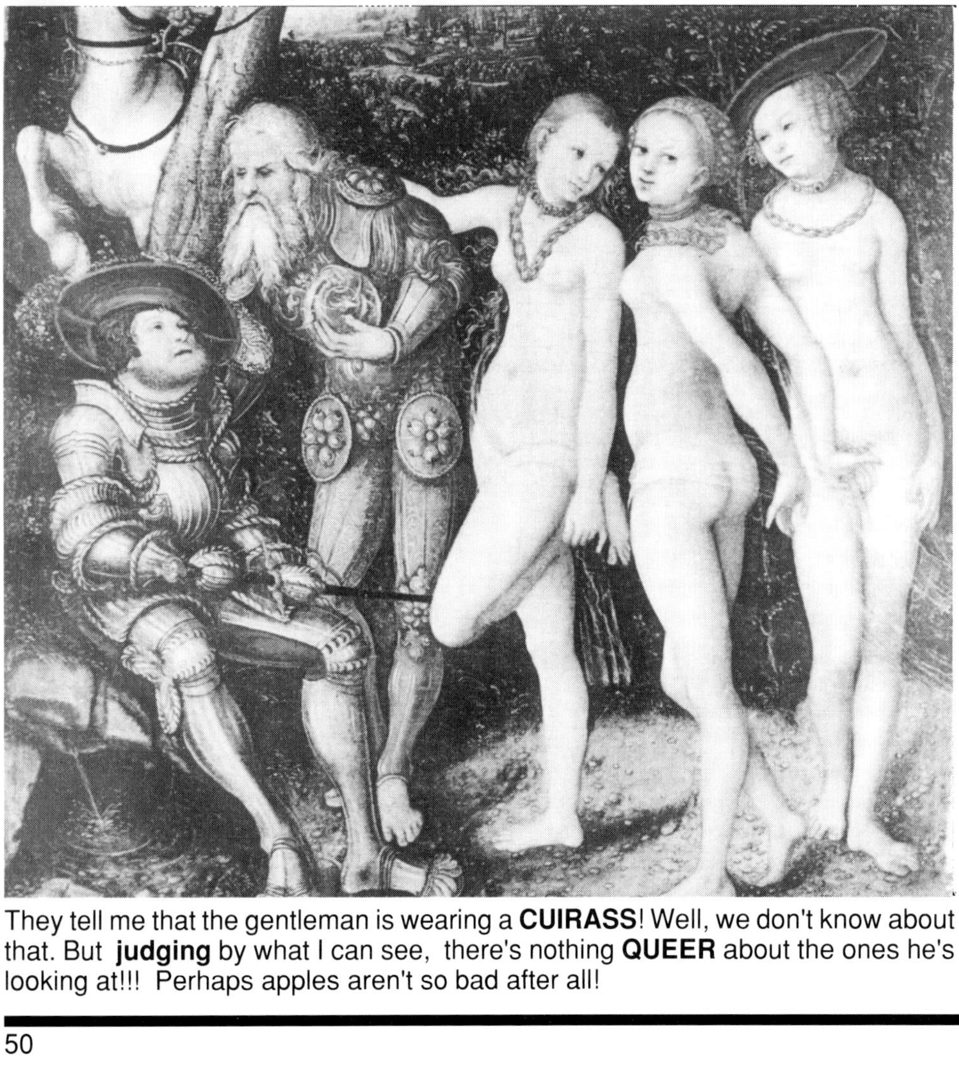

They tell me that the gentleman is wearing a **CUIRASS**! Well, we don't know about that. But **judging** by what I can see, there's nothing **QUEER** about the ones he's looking at!!! Perhaps apples aren't so bad after all!

NEWS FROM NORTH OF THE BORDER

You'll never guess what the old Jock King is up to these days!
We'll give you a clue: it's got something to do with spiders, something to do with sitting in a cave, and something to do with not knowing when you're beaten.
No wonder Hadrian built a wall to keep those crackpots out.
At least we've only got Millwall to worry about!

BIG S SHOW-BIZ S-PLEMENT

To mark the move of the Pope to Avignon, the Big S is offering, exclusively to its readers, a great new hit single by a great old folksinger:

Sur le pont d'Avignon by Lonnie Doncey, Lonnie Doncey!

BIG S IN-DEPTH INQUIRY

How much longer will this Dark Age last?
Who is responsible?
Will the plague make your breasts sag?

The Big S says: Something must be done. This is positively medieval

What a pong, Hong-Kong!!!

Now we've heard it all. Those little yellow chinkie people are trying to sell powder that burns!
They say, and don't laugh, folks, that you take a hollow iron tube and shove some of this powder down it, stuff a load of old knickers or pullovers in on top and then some old nails or horseshoes or something like that, and then you stick a match in the tube at the other end, there's a big bang and everything gets thrown all over the shop.
The Big S says it's just a craze.
So some spoilt rich kid is going to buy some and play around for a while, just like the Crusader's Cube, or the Holland Hoop, but it won't last. So try pulling the other one, little slant-eyed friends.
My kids make a bigger mess than that without trying, and **I can think of much better ways of getting a big bang.**

BIG S LITERARY S-PLEMENT

Those eye-ties are a rum lot. What do they do while the poor and the humble are dying in the streets in their millions?
They hot-foot it off to the mountains, and sit around in a luxury villa telling stories.
Yes, Boccaccio is making a fortune with the tales of a group of young people politely waiting (continued on page 9)

SUPER FUN BIG S COMPETITION SUPER FUN BIG S

Super Big S Black Death Competition WIN WIN WIN

They say it never rains but it pours, but if this little miss by the name of **Susie Rain** is anything to go by, it could pour on me as long as it liked.
Come on, Susie Rain, you could be my suzerain any time you like, and I could be your vassal!!!

COMPETITION SUPER FUN BIG S COMPETITION SUPER FUN BIG S COMPETITION SUPER FUN BIG S COMPETITION SUPER FUN BIG S COMPETITION SUPER FUN BIG

WHAT DO YOU THINK? Scratch your answers on a big lump of stone.
All Winners will receive a FREE SUPER BIG S SUPER-FUN-FUN-FUN-FUNERAL AT A NEIGHBOURHOOD LIMEPIT OF THEIR VERY OWN CHOICE!!!

SUPER FUN BIG S COMPETITION SUPER FUN BIG S COMPETITION SUPER FUN BIG S COMPETITION SUPER FUN BIG S COMPETITION SUPER FUN BIG S COMPETITION SUPER FUN BIG S COMPETITION SUPER FUN BIG

THE BIG S

THE BIG S BRINGS YOU THE HOTTEST LITTLE GIRL IN TOWN

Date: The Hundred Years War   Price: A bit of peace and quiet
Thought: Doesn't time fly when you're having fun?

WATCH IT, WELSHIES, OR WE'LL WALLOP YOU AGAIN.

This little dish strikes us as a bit of a sizzler even without the stake! A bit of crackling nice enough to make a rabbi's mouth water. And that's just the apple!

We've just about had enough of those Taffies.
We do not want to hear the name of Owen Glendower again, or the names of any of his sidekicks.
They just don't know how to play fair, those Taffs.
You conquer them and ask them if they've given in and they say "Yes" as nice as pie to your face, and then, the minute your back is turned, they turn round and start fighting again. So you go back over and "Please, Sir English Lord," they whine, "it wasn't me. It was Ianto, over by there."
So you go over and hang and draw and quarter Ianto and a few of his mates, do a regular little spot of raping and looting and pillaging and killing while you're in the area, and head off for home again, and no sooner do you get to Gloucester than they're at it again, revolting, whinging, little
(continued on page 7)

BIG S LITERARY S-PLEMENT ROYAL EXCLUSIVE

King's uncle scores a winner with red-hot tales of sex and lust and adultery!!!
Read all the naughty goings-on going on on the way to Canterbury!

Henry IV's uncle, Geoffrey Chaucer, tells it like it is!!!
And you can read it the way it is in the new super Big S super serial starting in the Big S on Monday.

SOMETHING'S BURNING!

Things hotted up in Rouen yesterday for that lovely little cooker Joan O'Farc.

VOICES

That little Maid in France won't be hearing any more voices in her ears, according to our reporter, for she was burned at the stake, much to the joy of everybody present.

PARLEZ-VOUS FRANCAIS, GRAND G?

After all, claiming to speak to Big G was really over the top, because she doesn't speak a word of English, and **we're pretty damn sure Big G didn't waste his time learning French just to go and whisper in her little garlic-stinking ear!**

A GOOD LESSON

Let's hope that we've all learned from this lesson and we don't make the same mistake again. Give a woman a bit of power and it goes to her head. They're more trouble than they're worth.

WOMEN IN THEIR PLACE

Don't get us wrong: we are not opposed to women as such. They have a very important place in society. We just want them to stay in that place! Let's face it, even the Army could not carry out its looting and pillaging and raping if there weren't any women!

But enough is enough. You can't let a woman take command of an army just because she hears voices in the night!

ASKED FOR IT

The Big S says those Froggies asked for everything they got!!!

P.S. Why has she got an Irish name?

THE BIG S

GUESS WHAT THEY'RE HAVING FOR CHRISTMAS DINNER IN CONSTANTINOPLE THIS YEAR!

Date: 1453 Price: One icon Thought: Here today, gone tomorrow.

WHOOPS A DAISY

CONSTANTINOPLE FALLS

That's the longest word you'll see in this paper. And no, it isn't a horse in the three-thirty.

Now, seriously, folks, after a thousand years of making his subjects fall flat on their faces whenever he went past, it's the Byzantine Emperor himself who's come a cropper this time.

Yes, Constantinople has fallen, and along with it the remains of the Byzantine Empire.

The Big S says: And not before time!!

BRAIN DRAIN STARTS AS SCHOLARS HOTFOOT IT TO THE WEST.

And it's not only the brains that are on the move. The Turks must have a serious social problem, because everybody moves out the minute they move in.

The most recent one to scarper was the niece of the Emperor who legged it to Moscow and quickly shacked up with Ivan III, sometimes called the Good, sometimes called the Great, and usually called something we can't print here!

But she must be quite some dish, because he's promised to build her a brand new palace, complete with domes and funny towers and lots of colours and gold and jewels, just like the one she left behind. They say they're going to call it the Kremlin. Now that's what we call paying a pretty high price for a bit of Eastern Promise. She must be a lot better than baklava!

NOBLE SAVAGES?

This luscious little lovely looks pretty noble to me, and we certainly wouldn't mind being savaged by her in the New World or the Old.

Thank goodness it's not only the Earth that's not flat, eh, fellas?

There's a really lovely King we've got by here now, isn't it, look you, boyo bach, indeed to goodness, thank you very much!

Wherever you go in London these days, there's some snivelling, grovelling little Taffie jabbering away, spitting all over the place, stinking of leek soup, and that's the King!!!

We didn't mean it, Henry: there's only joking we are, isn't it?

But seriously, though, it is getting a bit much. We didn't expect the Wars of the Roses to be won by a host of gobbling daffodils!

At this rate, we're beginning to regret that old Richard didn't find a taker when he was offering his kingdom for a horse.

At least horses are quite intelligent and have acceptable manners, whereas this Henry Tudor and his bunch of squabbling, jabbering, stinking, grasping, cheating, thieving, dragon-breathed

(continued on page 7)

The Big S says: There's sick it's beginning to make us , isn't it?

HEINEKEN'S DISEASE

MEDICAL WORLD BAFFLED

A new epidemic is spreading like wildfire throughout Europe, sparing neither rich nor poor, noble or slave, teacher or preacher, public figures or private parts.

It is commonly referred to as Heineken's disease, because it reaches the parts other diseases don't! This strange new phenomenon which is attacking the nation in its most vital areas is making our experts scratch their heads, while those afflicted with the disease are desperately scratching their

(continued on page 7)

ROYAL STORY EXCLUSIVE

THE BIG S HAS DONE IT!!!

TWO LITTLE PRINCES FOUND

In our SUPER SPECIAL BIG S EXCLUSIVE BIG S SUPER FUN ROYAL STORY we tell you how we found the two little princes.

We can now tell you that they are alive and well, living in Hull, and working with a super-fun bunch of knock-about strolling jesters, well-known in all the gayest

(continued on page 11)

THE BIG S

BIG S EXCLUSIVE ROMEO AND JULIET
Full colour gory etchings
page 9

Date: 1500 Price: One florin Thought: A new frock doesn't make a Renaissance

We could fancy having a go with this little Renaissance number! And they do say that things go better with a shell, don't they, fellas?

SOMETHING'S BURNING

Sour-puss Savvy goes up in smoke

Yes, old misery-guts Savonarola has gone. The bits of him that were left after his month's interrogation in the Papal prison were burned yesterday in the main square.
And the Big S says: Good riddance to bad rubbish.

So it's business as usual tonight! And we bet most of you will be letting your hair down after four years of fasting and not getting married and general misery!
Now it's back to the good bad old days of the Borgias, with their orgies and adulteries and feasting and raping and killing and stealing and plotting and conniving and incest and torture **and that's only the POPE!**

No, seriously, Al, we're only joking. It's great to have you back. - - And all our best to the wives and the kids!!!

HOW TO SUCCEED IN POLITICS WITHOUT REALLY TRYING

Yes, you too can be a great success in politics, become a powerful figure in your home town, and get all the girls you want!!!

READ MACHIAVELLI'S GRIPPING NEW SERIES IN THE BIG S

Are you cruel, ruthless, vicious, devoid of any sense of morality, totally self-centred, prepared to lie, cheat, torture, maim, and kill to protect your own position?

IF YOU CAN HONESTLY ANSWER YES TO THAT QUESTION THEN YOU TOO COULD BECOME PRIME MINISTER!!!

WHO'S A PRETTY BOY?

WHAT A LOT OF WOP ROT, BUONARROTI!!!

If you go down to the Vatican today, you're sure of a big surprise! All the little Palace poofters will be standing around in their new frocks, designed by well-known couturier, sculptor, painter, architect and habitué of gay drag bars, Michelangelo.

THEY'LL ALL BE HOLDING THEIR HALBERDS AND CHALLENGING EACH OTHER WITH A WHO GOES THERE, FWEND OR FWOE?

WOP PERVERT STEALS FROM THE BIG S.

Not only does he try to pass off as his own work a statue that **the Big S featured 2525 years ago**, but now old Angelface has been playing with the soldiers and dressing them up in their sister's clothes!!!

Such provocation is planned by Pope Al Borgia to keep media attention away from his own goings-on.

No wonder the eye-ties call the Pope "Papa"! They'll have to put up the taxes just to pay his family allowances.

Meanwhile, one of the Borgia Brats, luscious Lucretia, is getting through men faster than the Plague ever did! Perhaps that's why they dress up as women, to try and keep themselves safe!

And sonny Cesare is doing his bit to maintain the family tradition by bringing perversion back to Florence after the last few lean years, with a bit of help from Papa "Papa"!

THE BIG S

Date: 1521 | Price: One can of worms | Thought: We wish to protest

FANTASTIC FUNTASTIC BIG S-TASTIC COMPETITION

WIN AN INDULGENCE FOR A SIN OF YOUR CHOICE!

Sin and Win!

Yes, a Tetzel Tasty Special indulgence with the Pope's Personal Guarantee.

SIN NOW AND DON'T PAY LATER!

SEE PAGE 5!

You've heard about those foreign johnnies, Froggie poofters and Eye-tie idiots, eating all sorts of strange muck, like frogs and snails and horses and mushrooms, but now the Boche are at it!!!

DIET OF WORMS

No, we're only joking.

The po-faced Krauts may not be the happiest bunch around, but they haven't started eating worms yet!

It's old LULU LUTHER who's going to Worms, and that's the name of a town, not an intestinal complaint due to lack of personal hygiene!

It seems Lulu got a bit fed up with some of the malarkey going on in the church so he nailed up the door, burned a bull and is now being in

(continued on page 5)

STRIKE, STRANGLE, STAB SECRETLY OR IN PUBLIC!!!

LULU LUTHER may be mixed up in all sorts of skullduggery, but at least he's prepared to stand up for what is right when it comes to law and order and dealing with the peasants, who are even more revolting than usual at the moment over there in Bocheland.

"Strike, strangle, stab secretly or in public," he advises! "Hunt them down like mad dogs!" he urges.

The Big S says: Right on, Lulu! Enough is enough. The government must act now!

MAKE A MILLION

---------IN THE COMFORT OF YOUR OWN HOVEL!!!---------

WITH POPE LEO'S HOME PARTY RELICS AND INDULGENCES PLAN

Invite well-known sinners into your home, or invite people round to a sinful party, and then sell our genuine 100% guaranteed RELICS AND INDULGENCES.

YOU COULD MAKE A MILLION and have any sins committed in the course of work forgiven FREE OF CHARGE

See the Big S SUPER FUN SPECIAL EXCLUSIVE INTRODUCTORY OFFER on page 9!!!

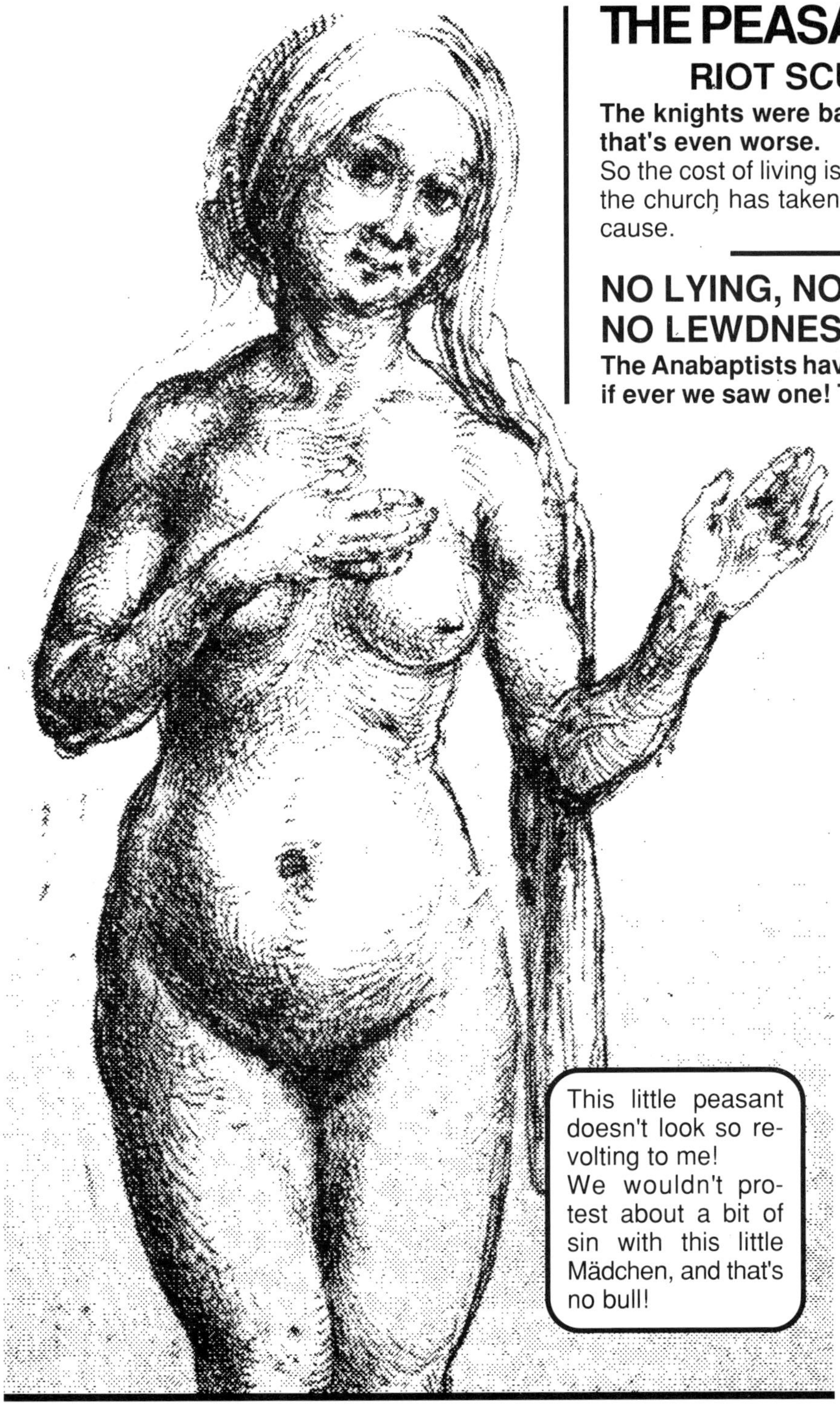

THE PEASANTS ARE REVOLTING

RIOT SCUM MUST BE SMASHED

The knights were bad enough, but now it's the peasants and that's even worse.

So the cost of living is going up: that's the same for everybody. So the church has taken over all of the land, but that's all for a good cause.

NO LYING, NO SWEARING, NO GLUTTONY, NO LEWDNESS, NO BOOZINESS

The Anabaptists have come up with a vote-catching manifesto if ever we saw one! The loony left says the end of the world is nigh, and if that's the sort of world they want, then the end can't come fast enough.

The Big S says they're all Pinko-poof-ter-party-poopers!

A handful of ignorant peasants are led on by their promises of no taxes, no military service and communal ownership of all property, but they'd soon change their minds if they ever got into power and had

(continued on page 5)

EVEN MORE FANTASTIC FUNTASTIC BIG S-TASTIC COMPETITION

Win the Head of John the Baptist, beautifully preserved in a specially designed cut glass bowl.

Runners-up get pieces of the shin-bone of the ass that carried old what's-his-name into Jerusalem!!!

THE BIG S

BIG S ROYAL SHOWBIZ SPECIAL

Henry's great hit number, GREENSLEEVES, moves to number ONE in the charts, toppling Hey Nonny Nonny No which has been at number one for the last 85 years.

Date:1536, but we're not counting, Henry. Honest. Price Who cares? Honest, we're not counting.
Thought: Two heads are better than one, but we're not counting.

HENRY HAS ANOTHER GO

ANOTHER ROYAL WEDDING EXCLUSIVE!

CITY BONANZA AS TRADE FIGURES SOAR

City businessmen are rubbing their hands with glee. They've sold more mugs and plates and headscarfs since Our Henry came to the throne than in the last two centuries put together!

What with Royal Weddings, and Royal Divorces and Royal Births and Royal Funerals, they are having the time of their lives. And now that Royal Executions are becoming so popular, they have a nifty little number in souvenir miniature axes at one farthing each.

BIG S ROYAL PORTRAIT SUPER SNEAK PREVIEW

Our reporter managed yesterday to get a sneak look at the new Royal portrait being painted by Hans Holbein, well-known Kraut portrait painter on all the best pavements in London.

We know that our gracious and splendidly slim King is taking great interest in this painting after his earlier disappointments. "I just hope," Henry confided to our reporter, "that this Boche fellow doesn't make me look like a fat old queen like that other fellow did, you know, the one whose head came off."

The Big S says: Hey, Hans, if you don't want to be a very sour Kraut, I'd take it easy on the paint round the waistline.

SUPER BIG S SCIENCE SPECIAL S-PLEMENT

Now, readers, hold on tight or you might fall off!!!
There's this old Pole, Copernicus, who is a bit keen on **heliocentricity!** How about that for a word?
No, that isn't what the Egyptians used to use to write with. It means that we're going round the Big S every day at a speed that would make even **our** readers' minds boggle.

This old Pole is right up the Pole!!
We know that it's worth going to a lot of effort to get the Big S every day, but we still don't expect you to run round the whole world at tens of miles an hour.
Can you imagine the mess it would make of your hair, not

(continued on page 7)

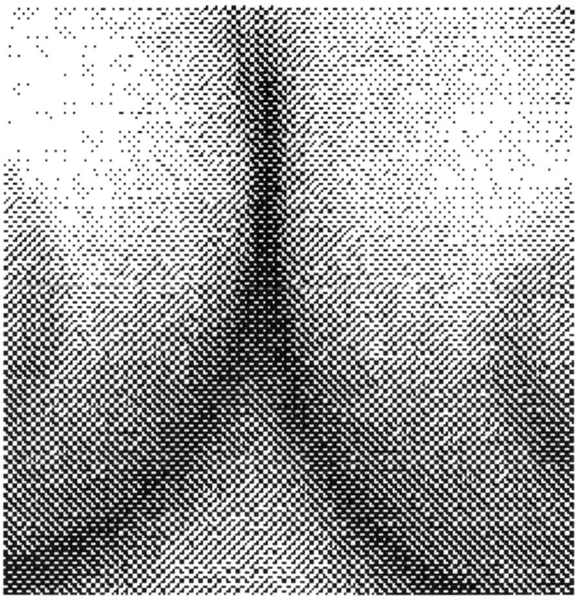

On the right, Copernicus' idea of celestial orbs!

On the left, well, if you <u>need</u> telling, there's <u>no point</u> in telling.

We just know you'd have to be pretty keen on heliocentricity, or perhaps rather prone to eccentricity to prefer the concentricity.

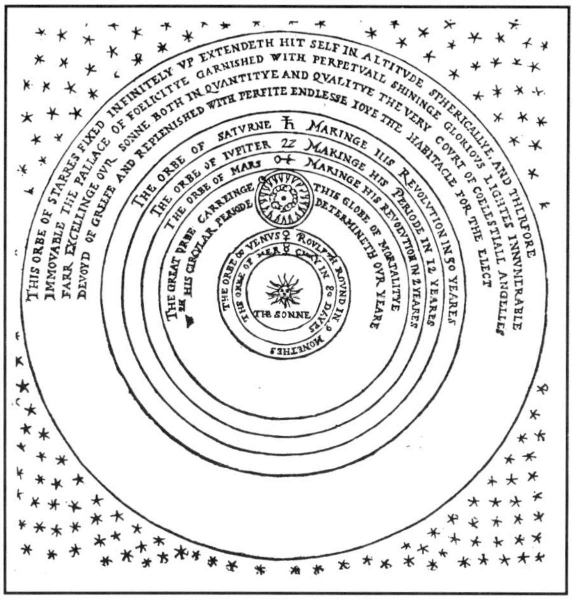

EXCITING BIG S SUPER READER OFFER

As a part of the great public celebration of the Royal Executions, The BIG S has commissioned from LEADING ENGLISH ARTISTS AND CRAFTSMEN a series of ABSOLUTELY EXQUISITE little SOUVENIR HEADS in *fine English Bone China*.

Each jewel-like head is hand-decorated in glowing life-like colours at only TWO PENCE EACH, or 35 guineas the set. Be careful, this offer is strictly limited to one per hovelhold and is for a limited period only.

GREAT SEVERED HEADS OF ENGLAND.

Collectors can subscribe to the Great Severed Heads of England suite by signing up and receiving one head a month, personally delivered and packed, at NO EXTRA CHARGE, in its own craftsman designed commemorative basket.

THIS MONTH'S ISSUE IS THAT VIVACIOUS LITTLE CUTIE ANNE BOLEYN, HER BLACK EYES AND LONG CURLY HAIR LOVINGLY RECREATED BY THE TIME-HONOURED TRADITIONAL ARTS OF OUR GREAT NATION.

Future issues may include statesmen, philosophers, cardinals, queens, princes, famous criminals and/or Prime Ministers, artists who make Him look too fat in their paintings, anybody whose song gets to number one in the hit-parade and topples Greensleeves, anybody who jostles Him in the toilets, anybody who says that Jeanne Seymour can't act and should stick to soap commercials, Italian tourists, Catholics, Scots, Irish, French, Germans, anybody richer than Him, any other foreigners, people who keep count of

(continued on page 5,6,7,8,9)

THE BIG S

Date: 1588 Price: One colony Thought: It will never catch on

GOVERNMENT HEALTH WARNING

POTATOES MAY BE BAD FOR YOUR HEALTH

How beauteous mankind is!
O brave new world,
that has such people in't!
Anon

FRANKIE GOES TO HO!

Francis Drake on the Costa del Shipwreck!

There'll be lots of new fun things for the kids to do down at the seaside this year: discovering shipwrecks, diving for pieces of eight, finishing off drowning or injured Spanish sailors!

We'd heard that they had some lovely 'taters over there, and if this is what Wally is bringing back, then all is forgiven. It may be a New World, but thank goodness some of the old places look very familiar!

South coast resorts are looking forward to a bumper fun year.

Francis Drake took time off from a game of bowls to dash out and demolish the Navy of Spanish loony Philip this weekend.

And he was back on the green to win by three ends with a marvellous last wood, beautifully weighted, that curled right around the defences put up by his opponent and came to rest nestling poetically against the Jack.

We don't suppose the Spanish king is too happy about it all, but we don't really care about that! He earned himself the nickname of Philip the Pillock when he said he would personally burn his own son

(continued on page 3)

GREAT SEVERED HEADS OF ENGLAND!

This month's issue:

MARY QUEEN OF SCOTS, number 11,478 in our BIG S SUPER SOUVENIR CELEBRITY CERAMIC SERIES

Order form on page 6

WALTER RALEIGH IS THE 11-4 ON FAVOURITE FOR NEXT MONTH'S CELEBRITY SUPERSTAR EXECUTION.

See inside for odds on other contenders!!

YOU WALLY, WALLY!

The Big S says: if that's what the New World does to you, Wally, then you'd better leave it alone.

People say that travel broadens the mind, but it doesn't seem to have done much for poor old Walter Raleigh.

Our reporter has heard that Queen Lizzie was not too amused when old Wally came rushing up to the palace after another jaunt over to the New World and offered her a fag.

HIS WORST JOKE SINCE NAMING THE COLONY VIRGINIA!!!

We don't know just how unamused she was, but a messenger did send Wally's pyjamas and toothbrush back from the Palace, and a man with a black hood over his head has been seen taking his neck measurement!

Lizzie was no doubt expecting something more in the line of things that the Spanish Queen gets: gold, silver, or jewels, not a packet of fags, a couple of spuds and something that old Wally calls a bicycle

QUEEN STUMPED

The tobacco and the potatoes were hard enough to sort out, but nobody's managed to figure out what to do with the bicycle yet.

The Queen's first attempt caused a certain physical discomfort, not to mention acute embarrassment, when she

(continued page 5)

THE BIG S

Date:1605   Price: Everything you've got, sucker!   Thought: It will all be forgotten by next week.

ROYAL PRATT SPECIAL

THE KING CLAIMS DIVINE RIGHT!

THESE PURITANS ARE A PAIN IN THE POSTERIOR

The Big S says: If you feel like that, why don't you pack up and push off somewhere else?

Let somebody else put up with them for a change. They're always moaning. Moan, moan, moan, moan, moan.

After all, it's one thing complaining about the King's stupidity, but it's no good if you're just as stupid yourself.

These Separatists with their ideas on purity and morality and not doing this and not doing that and sin and punishment would make life absolute hell, and they'd still tell us that's where we were going next anyway!!!

SUPER BIG S SUPER SHOWBIZ SPECIAL —— THEATRE ——

MACBETH MAKETH US YAWN

There's yet another tedious tale of skullduggery at the Globe as Wee Willie Shakespeer tries to curry a spot of Royal favour with this tiresome tale of nastiness up in the land of the Jocks.

The Big S says: if that's the best you can do, Willie, it's time to pack it in and go back to the wife and kids in Leeds.

WITTY DITTIES AND PRETTY BOYS

Meanwhile, across town, a super night was had at the opening of a new musical by Andy Floyd Leper, **Who's that in your doublet?** There are many memorable ditties, a witty script, simply gorgeous costumes, and a jaunty air about the whole production, all coming to a climax as the audience joined in the final rousing chorus of Tara-diddle-diddle-diddle-fol-de-rol-de-rol.

And judging by the number of people whistling this tune as they left the theatre, this is going to be another SMASH HIT FOR ANDY.

The Big S says: this is what theatre should be like. Eat your heart out, Willie.

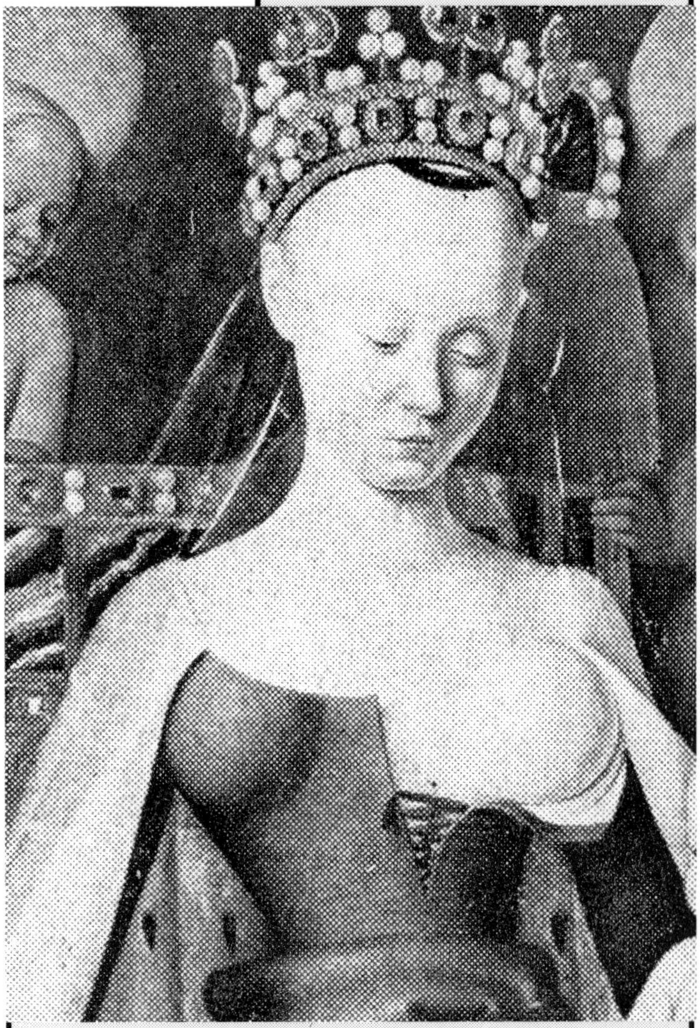

THE BIG S says:

WE'RE SURE WE DON'T KNOW ABOUT THE KING'S DIVINE RIGHT, BUT WE SURE KNOW A DIVINE LEFT WHEN WE SEE ONE!

NICE TRY, GUY!

Members of Parliament who were grappling with the serious matters of State last night were almost woken up when Guy Fawkes nearly managed to do what most of us would like to do: blow up the Houses of Parliament along with all its members!

BIGGEST BANG OF THEIR LIVES

Members of Parliament usually abuse their power and position to obtain all sorts of things -company directorships, jobs at a university, girls, sinecures as heads of recently privatised national undertakings.

But last night they almost got the biggest bang of their lives without having to resort to bribery and coercion.

JAMES THE RIDICULOUS

Guy and a couple of cronies wanted to do us all a favour by getting rid of Jumped-up James the Ridiculous!

The Big S says this is going too far.

So James **has** increased taxes, **is** a conceited oaf, **does** think he's the greatest thing until they invent sliced bread, **does** go round saying that he is like a god and can do no wrong, **doesn't** take the slightest bit of notice of anybody who has an opinion different to his, **does** stick his nose into everything, especially into things he knows nothing about -and that's most things- **but is that any reason for trying to blow him up?**

There's nothing new in any of that.

That's what you expect of Kings and Princes and politicians and Prime Ministers, and we can't go round blowing them all up, can we?

THE BIG S

SUPER BIG S BLACK AND WHITE S-PLEMENT

Date: 1649 | Price: Half a crown | Thought: All change.

NATURAL SCIENCE

Eye-tie loony reckons we're on the move.

It must be the heat that does it down in the land of the Wop, but Galileo Galilei has dug up the old idea that the earth is whizzing round and round!!! These foreign johnnies don't give up, do they? Mind you, when we tell you that poor Galileo's other great interest is rushing up the Tower of Pisa and dropping his balls over the edge to see if they fall to the ground, you will see that poor old GG is a few bricks short of a load.

The Big S says come on, GG, tell us what else is new in the land of spaghetti.

FRACAS BETWEEN ROUNDHEADS AND CAVALIERS

The tranquil sea-side village of Brighton was perturbed yesterday when a group of long-haired, loose-living Cavalier youths poured into town intent on conflict with the roundheads, local boys much given to the study of the Scriptures, with nice short hair, sober clothing and clean finger-nails -a model of sobriety and clean living and

(continued on page 9)

ARTS AND LETTERS

Rene Descartes has galvanised philosophers throughout the civilised world with his startling new ideas on the modes of human existence.

Descartes philosophizing

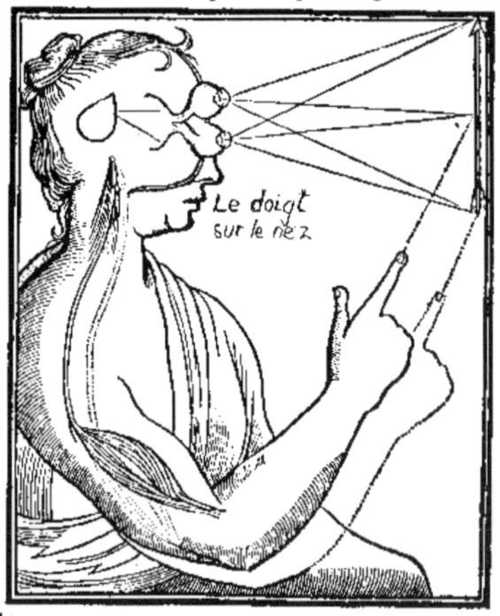

The Big S says that this little Froggy has quite definitely put his **DESCARTES** in front of his **DES-HORSE!!**!

"I think, therefore I am!!!" says Rene in his new book.

Maybe, Froggy, but we wouldn't like to say just what you are.

Carry on thinking, snail-eater, but do us a favour and keep it to yourself.

Beauty is in the eye of the beholder, and we'd behold these little beauties any time at all, wouldn't we, brethren?

SO LONG IT'S BEEN GOOD TO KNOW YOU

WE DON'T THINK!

Praise the Lord, companions and fellow believers. Our Ollie has socked it to him at last.

Charlie I was beheaded at Whitehall yesterday and now it's Long Live Ollie.

The Big S says: good riddance to bad rubbish.

That's the last we'll see of dictators and divine right and kings and nobles and all their parasitic flunkies!

After the excesses of recent years, the Big S is looking forward to an age of sobriety, of propriety, of purity, of integrity, of morality, of proper respect for those things worthy of respect, to a new age where the righteous shall inher-

(continued on page 7)

THE BIG S

Date: Just a little later | Price: One orange | Thought: Plus ça change ...

SHOWBIZ SPECIAL

Win two tickets to the sensational new musical now drawing the crowds in London.

HELLO, CHARLIE

opens at the Drury Lane. See the show and whistle along with the great hit song,

"IT'S SO NICE TO SEE YOU BACK WHERE YOU BELONG"

WHAT GOES UP MUST COME DOWN

The Big S, in an exclusive interview with the author of a sensational new book, brings you the latest low-down on the new-fangled theory of gravity.

"Every particle of matter," Isaac told our special science reporter in his garden this week, where he was recuperating after an unfortunate encounter with an apple, "every particle of matter in the universe attracts every other particle with a force varying inversely as the square of the distance between them and directly proportional to the product of their masses."

The Big S says that that's all well and good as far as it goes, but don't forget everything's relative. Try and keep indoors until the swelling goes down, Isaac.

BIG S SUPER SPECIAL SUPER FUN SUPER SCIENCE S-PLEMENT part two

BEGONIAS DO BONK AFTER ALL!

Well, if you go down in the woods today, you might get a big surprise!
It seems that the plants are all at it after all, despite old Aristotle.

Randy dandy Eyetie Marcello Malpighi reveals all in the Super Fun Exclusive Big S guide to the secret sex life of the plants!

All this week! **Only in the Super Big S**

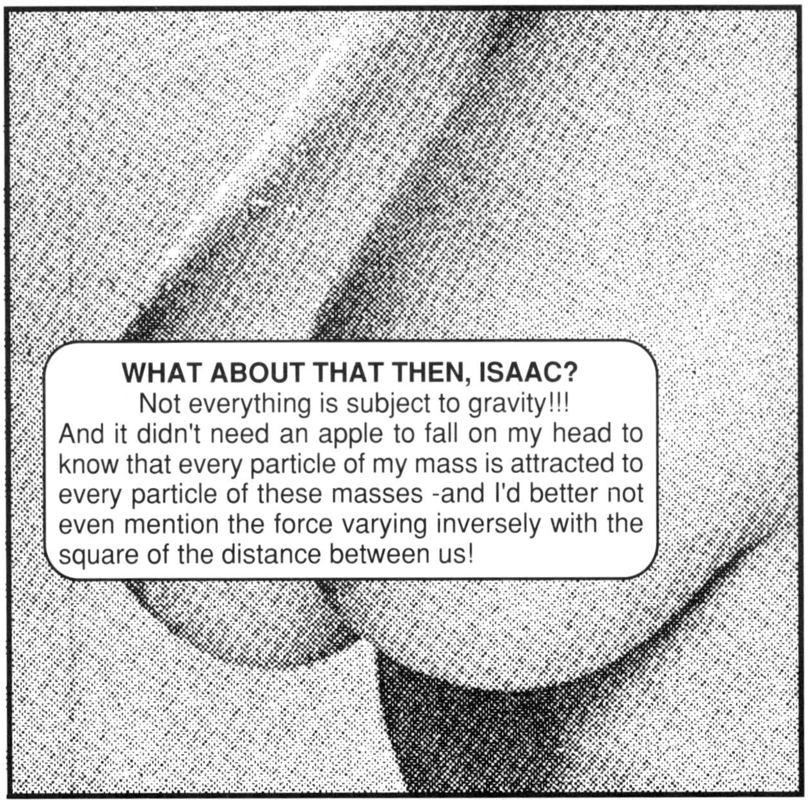

NOT ON YOUR NELLY

No wonder the sale of choc ices is dropping off after the boom during the recent fire in the capital city! This saucy little number is doing a roaring trade selling her oranges in all the best places these days.

The Big S also hears that she's also selling quite a few of her best places as well, but that's another story.

Yes, little Nellie Gwynne has been made Purveyor of Fruit by Appointment to his Majesty, and we're not surprised at all. Charlie has got a divine right, and it takes one to spot one. No, seriously, though, Nell was selling her oranges and lemons near Saint Clement's, and the display of her wares, especially since her wares were'nt wearing much, could not fail to catch the royal eye (or should that be the royal we?).

The Big S says Nell's got lovely oranges, and quite a smashing pear!

SUPER FUN SUPER BIG S SUPER COMPETITION.

Come on, readers, have a go.

Join in our fun competition and forget about that miserable fire! It's no use sitting round playing with the embers.

DESIGN A NEW CATHEDRAL FOR LONDON.

Entries on a postcard please by next Friday.

THE BIG S

Read the stars in the Big S!
We predict that the INDUSTRIAL REVOLUTION is about to start!
Only in the Big S! This week!
See p 9

Date: 1746 Price: Two haggis Thought: The best laid schemes o'mice an' men gang aft a-gley

SUPER FUN SUPER BIG S "SOCK IT TO THE SCOTS"

SPECIAL ISSUE

Super Big S-clusive Super Witchcraft Special

"If you don't believe in witches, you don't believe in the Bible," writes our hard-hitting religious correspondent John "Burn-'em-all" Wesley on page 11.

PLUS PLUS PLUS

1001 WAYS TO HAVE FUN AT YOUR LOCAL COVEN'S ORGIES!

What to wear and what not to wear!
How to tell a virgin!!
Full exciting details on page 9!!!

DOUBLE, DOUBLE, TOIL AND TROUBLE;
FIRE BURN AND CAULDRON BUBBLE.
Scottish ladies looking for eye of newt, and toe of frog!

SEE INSIDE OUR STOP PRESS LATEST MEDICAL REPORT:
CRAZED COLONIAL QUACK INFECTS NEW ENGLANDERS WITH SMALLPOX IN CALLOUS EXPERIMENT

BIG S SPORT

ENGLAND WIN CULLODEN CUP OUTRIGHT

GOTCHA JOCK!

What a right Charlie!

The latest match in the series between England and Scotland ended in triumph when England won the Culloden cup.

REAL THRASHING

They gave Scotland a real thrashing and pulled even further ahead in the series which they now lead by 4 wins to 2. England have beaten teams led by Charles I, James II, James Stuart and now Charles Stuart, while James I and Charles II have scored for Scotland.

SCOTS CAPTAIN LEAVES IN HUFF!!!
UNAVAILABLE FOR INTERVIEW

The Scots captain, **Bonnie Prince Charlie**, left immediately after the match and refused to speak to our reporter. He had decided to follow in the family footsteps and do a quick bunk over the water!

He was last seen heading into the sunset on a boat rowed by a bunch of drunken supporters, who kept shouting "Onwards!", and singing some garbled rubbish about bonnie boats flying like birds in the sky.

The Big S says: good riddance. Let's hope that he will no come back again!

SCOT SCIENCE BIG S-PLEMENT

Wee Jimmy Jock Watt Wastes Days Watching Water

Poor Mrs Watt!

Her son Jimmy "Jock" Watt hangs around all day in the kitchen fiddling with the kettle.

"I'm at my wit's end," she confided to our reporter yesterday. "He's nearly ten now and should be out doing an honest day's work down the mine like his wee brothers and sisters. I swear that one of these days if he doesn't get up off his backside and stop playing with the kettle, I'll fetch him a right one round the

(continued on page 7)

Big S Super Fun Super Special Exclusive Offer

Buy our SPECIAL FUN SUPER STEAM KETTLE and make a Fortune.

Offer limited to one per hovel.

THE BIG S

JOIN OUR SUPER BIG S FUN CAMPAIGN

SAVE THE DODO

Date: A very g'day Price: A big pile of dingo's do. Thought: Too many Cooks spoil the broth

END OF WORLD DISCOVERED

"What a tip," Captain Cook complained to our reporter. "The first place I came to was so awful that I called it New South Wales. And the second, well, I mean, if you'd seen the fellows out on the beach, holding hands and ..., and..., well, anyway I decided to call it Queensland. And the people out here are terrible. I've only met one nice man, a fellow called Sydney, and I have very fond memories of him. Perhaps I'll call somewhere after him as well."

ALL THE GOOD PLACES ALREADY DISCOVERED.

"It's just not fair," he continued. "All the good places have already been discovered, places like Hudson's Bay and Tierra del Fuego and Tristan da Cunha. I mean, the history books are not going to be very kind to me for finding this dump, are they? It's just too horrid -apart from Sydney, of course- with animals that spend all their time jumping up and down, and people throwing sticks at each other and knocking themselves out, and there's another animal with a great, flat mouth like a duck's bill and with two

(continued on page 9)

The Big S says: Thank you, Captain Cook. What a chance to get rid of all our rubbish for ever!

BIG S SPORT: AUSTRALIAN FOOTBALL CUP FINAL

New South Wales 18 dead, 57 injured, Queensland 36 dead 156 injured.

There was a thrilling climax to the year's sporting activity this week when New South Wales hung on to the Australian Football Cup when Queensland submitted after 8 minutes of play.

New South Wales really were in devastating form, viciously attacking and maiming their opponents even before the kick-off. The coach had told our reporter before the game that they had been working hard on the set pieces, but you could hardly have expected such wholesale and rigorous slaughter before the beer can had even been touched by the other team.

Their centre forward made a dazzling run through the centre of the pitch, personally accounting for seven dead and five serious injuries in the first thirty seconds!!!

Queensland tried to fight back, but they were really outclassed and fully deserved the name given to them by Captain Cook on his recent visit.

Annual meeting of the Australian Arts Council

Now we know why they pronounce it ASS-tralia!!!

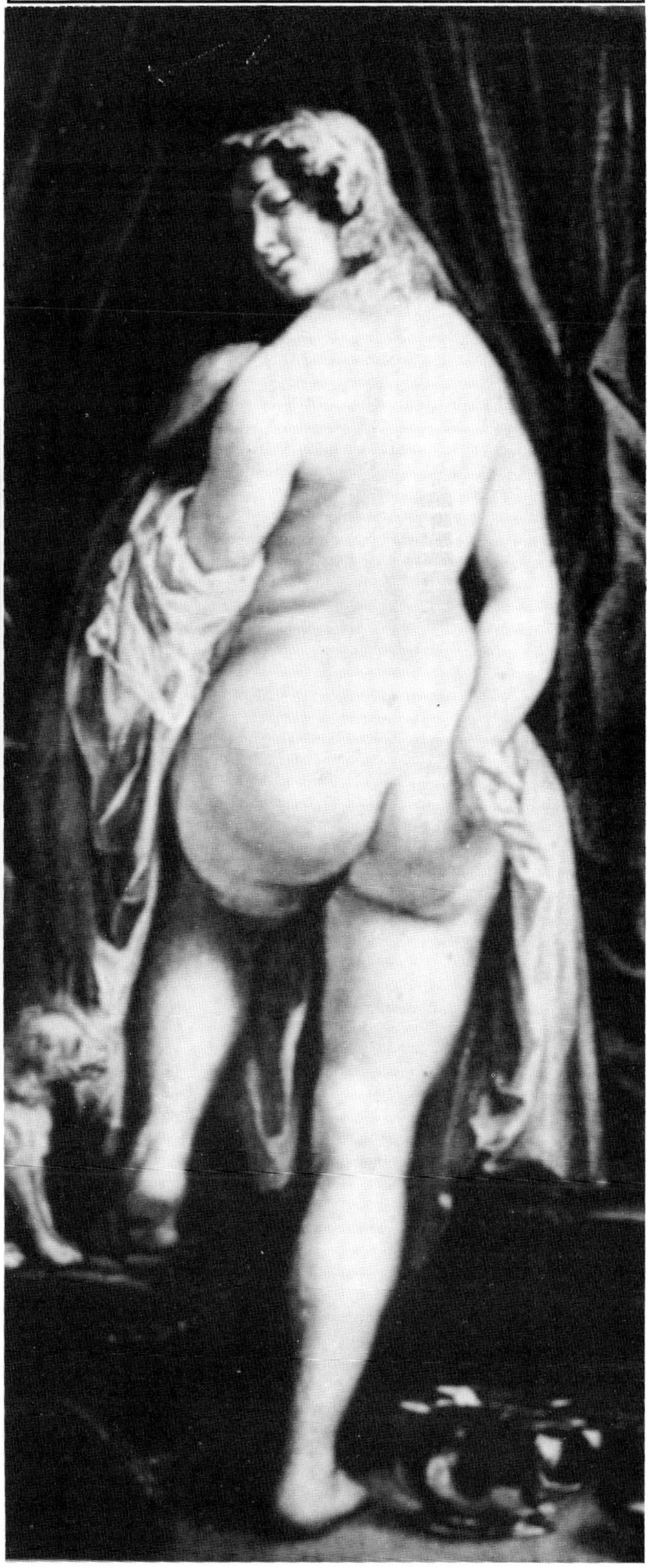

Literary Big S-plement

It's the latest craze down under in the land of the wallabies.

Imagine a bunch of morons in some up-market hovels, endlessly going into each other's kitchens to discuss continental quilt covers and recipes for kangaroo steaks!
Did you say that nothing could be that bad?
Just wait until you actually experience the latest Aussie hit serial to entrance the local yokels.
No description could be bad enough to do it justice.
It is to mind decay what sugar is to teeth! And the music is even worse!! Compared to fetid dingos' do, "The People next door"

(continued page 7)

THE BIG S

PLAY UP PAY UP AND PLAY THE GAME

Date: They can't even count over there! Price: A couple of beans.
Thought: Time for a nice cup of tea

THE BRITISH ARE COMING

SO JUST WATCH IT, YANKEES!

And let's hear no more of this rubbish!! Taxation without representation always has been, is now and always will be one of the cornerstones of the Great British way of life! How do you expect all our lords and ladies and dukes and princes and sirs and earls and so on and so on and so on and so on to be able to live like lords and ladies if they can't keep taking money from the poor? Taxation is essential. Even a poor colonial cretin should be able to understand that.

As for representation, don't make us laugh!

Why ask the poor if they want the rich to take their bit of money. Of course they don't. It's common sense. So why ask? Because we're going to take it anyway.

The Big S says: come on, lads: you've had a bit of fun and thrown the tea in the water, and you've marched up and down and impressed the girlies. But let's stop now before somebody gets hurt! Because if you don't, there'll be trouble! We're all English and proud of it, aren't we, fellas?

COLONIAL EDITION

VANDALS DEVASTATE CHERRY ORCHARD!

"It wasn't me, Mam. Honest," says chief suspect. Details on page 11.

SUPER BIG S SHOWBIZ SPECIAL

Continental Congress of Colonial Comedians held in Philadelphia!!

Shrieks of jollity and gales of laughter were heard issuing from the Continental Congress this weekend, reports our colonial correspondent.

"Have you heard the one about all men being created equal," spluttered a slightly inebriated Thomas Jefferson, struggling to his feet and fighting to control his mirth.

"Leave it out, Tom," giggled Ben "Burro" Franklin, "they'll never believe that. Have you ever been to Millwall?"

"I know, I know," chortled Bill Paca, "what about this one? This is a real screamer: 'Governments exist to secure the rights of the people, deriving their power from the consent of the governed' and then you put in something about unalienable rights!!!"

"Shut up and sit down, you nutter," called out John Adams, "there's always some pratt who has to go too far. Anyway," he added with a scowl, "what the hell kind of name is Paca? Who let a bloody ..."

(continued on page 7)

THE BIG S SAYS: TEACH THEM A LESSON! LET THEM TRY! THEY'LL SOON BE SORRY AND COME CRAWLING BACK!

If this is how Liberty leads the people, then we're not surprised they're so easily led. And not necessarily by the nose, eh, fellas?

We'd vote for this constitution any day of the week.
We certainly wouldn't say no to being united with this statuesque little scorcher.

THE BIG S

ZEE EEZ

Date: The First of the Windy month   Prix: 1 Crown   Pensee: Laissez les manger le gateau!

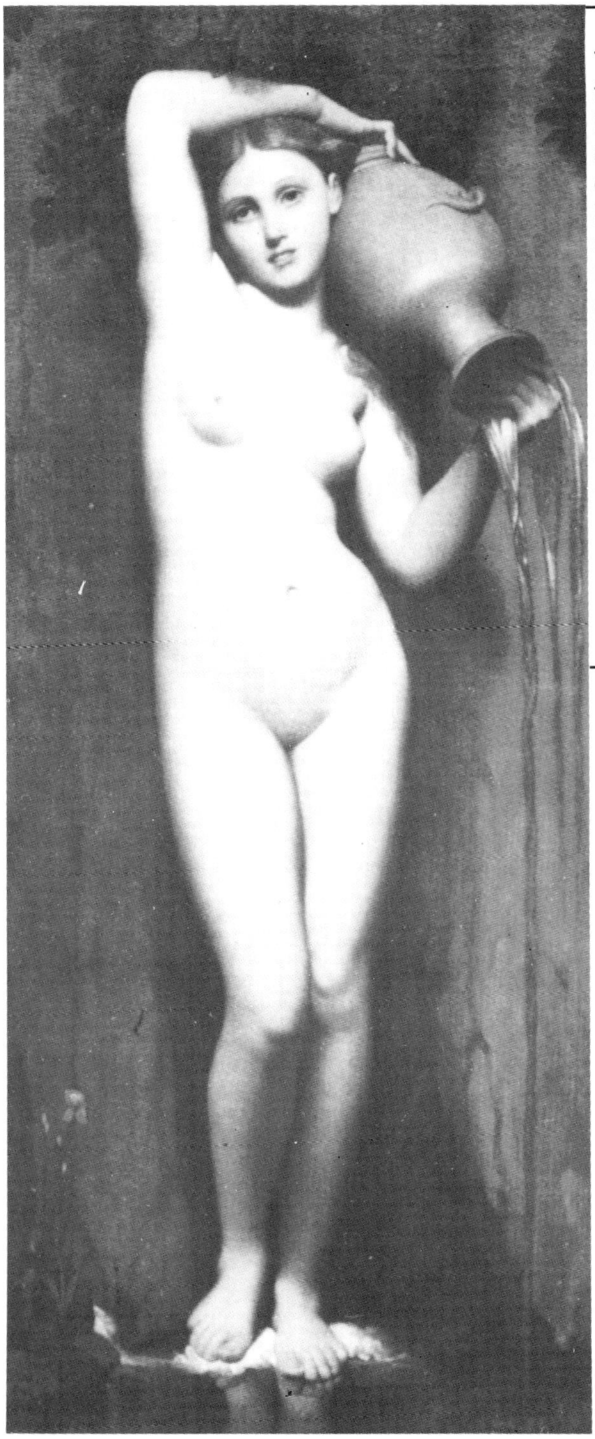

IRMA LA DOUCHE

The Frogs have never been too fond of water, for either internal or external application, and the common man's concern with personal hygiene has become even less pressing since little Charlotte stopped Danton playing with his rubber duck in the bath by parting the hair on his chest with a meat cleaver!

But we're glad to see that this little Mademoiselle has found a nice way to freshen up after a hard day's chopping off of heads.

If she was ever without, we'd let her have our choppers any day of the week, n'est-ce pas, les garçons?

Big S Science Special

Inveterate inventor strikes again!

And that doesn't mean he's very old, but that he can't stop doing it!!! We can understand that, can't we? We always say, if you can get it, do it!!!

Now seriously, folks, this latest brainwave of Dr Guillotine is set to sweep the world.

ZEE WORKMATE is a kind of small, folding table with lots of holes in it and legs that keep falling over and little handles to turn to make it bigger, except that the hole in the middle then gets bigger as well.

"I haven't thought of a use for it yet," said Dr Guillotine, "but I'm sure I will one day. Anyway it's only a question of **le marketing**, as we say in French. I'm also working on this great idea for a cheese cutter. You put the cheese on a tray, balance a sharp blade over it, let the blade go, et voilà, propre comme un whistle! Of course, the market for high tech

(continued on page 3)

Super Fun Super Big S Super Competition

Invent something really really useless! Judge: Dr Guillotine

ROYAL LITTERAIRE EXCLUSIF S-PLEMENT

Extraits du diary du King Louis!!!
Par exemple: "14/7/89: Nothing."

Readez that et beaucoup of other things interestings et excitings dans LE GRAND S this week.

FROGGIES REVOLTANT

Alors, sacre bleu et allo, allo!

Zee French froggies are at it again! Ouvrez la porte, they shout with garlic ridden breath, and off come the heads!!! Oh, la, la!!!

Oui, le peuple, this time, writes our special Parisian correspondent, zee Froggies really are revolting.

First it was the Bastille. Now there isn't an axe left in the shops, and the undertakers are making a fortune making tres beaucoup of shorter-than-average coffins.

The Big S says: if you can keep your head when all about you are losing theirs, then you're not a Froggie toff!

WE SAW YOUR KNICKERS!

There was great excitement today in the Place de la Bastille when Marie-Antoinette popped in for an appointment with the revolutionary hairdresser. He is, so everybody says, a little wonder with his axe and bucket and shovel.

"You have one of my cuts," his business card states proudly, "and you will never go elsewhere!"

QUEEN'S FIRST APPEARANCE

This was the first time the Queen had been seen in public for ages, and she had really made an effort for the big day! She looked stunning! But then, when she had mounted the platform and put her head on the block, A **SUDDEN GUST OF WIND BLEW, and we got an eyeful of some right royal dessous! Oh la la! White and frilly and very very ancien regime.**

Le Grand S dit: Vivent les French knickers!

THE BIG S

Date: 1815 Price: One delusion Thought: Howzat, Bony? 100 all out.

FUN FUN FUN

SUPER BIG S SPECIAL SPECTACULAR COMPETITION

LADIES!!!

WIN THIS SENSATIONAL PRIZE!

WIN A PAIR OF WELLINGTON BOOTS SIGNED BY THE DUKE HIMSELF!!!

Win this year's dazzling fashion accessory and do your bit for a great man.

NOT TONIGHT JOSEPHINE

I've had a terrible day at the battle!

You'd think the Froggies would have learned by now. You'd think they would see that they were NEVER going to win and that they should give up. But no! They keep coming back for more, and we have to give them another thrashing! If it weren't such good fun, you'd get tired of beating them up!

Old Bony won't be bonking tonight! The little Froggie midget turned up at Waterloo today but he didn't reckon on the good old Duke of Wellington.
So now he's waiting for the 18.15 to Saint-Helena with a one-way ticket in his hand!!

The Big S says: that's Bony's second innings over. Let's hear no more of that little laddie.

NO MORE WAR!!!
SIGNED SEALED & DELIVERED

A GOOD CHAT

All over Europe people have been celebrating the dawn of a new age as the rulers of Europe have got together and sat down and had a really good chat about things.

JUSTICE, CHARITY AND PEACE!

Yes, that's the order of the day. All nations dealing with each other with peace, goodwill and charity. It's all down on paper and signed on the dotted line.

It just needed that filthy Frog and his garlic-stinking mob out of the way for civilised people to sort it all out!

So let that be a lesson to any other lousy foreigner who thinks he can tell us how to keep the peace!

Otherwise, we can always nip round to your place and show you just what we mean by the Pax Britannica!

Josephine sulking about Bony's lack-lustre and lack-lust performance at Waterloo!

UP AND ATOM, JOHNNIE!

Now we've heard it all!!!

John Dalton says the world is made up of little bits of things whizzing round and making all sorts of other things **that aren't really there!**

The Big S says:
Why don't you go and live with the Froggies, John? They've got ways of dealing with nutters like you.

WHOSE IDEA WAS THIS, ANYWAY?

It was a stupid idea in the first place and the Big S says that whoever thought of it should own up and take the blame!!!

What an idea! Fancy letting Ireland be part of Britain! At the first touch of famine, they'll be creeping out of their bogs and coming over here! Then they'll want hovels to live in and property values will really come crashing down. Respectable slums will be nothing but an endless round of "Top of the morning" and "Begorrah" and drinking and squabbling.

They ought to think themselves lucky that we let them stay in Ireland!

It would be different if they all looked like Miss O'Murphy here, whose 'taters are appreciated far and wide.

THE BIG S

BIG S SUPER FUN BIG S-CLUSIVE SUPER FUN SEX SCANDAL

"THERE ARE NO GAY GEORGE GORDONS ROUND HERE!" says saucy sis Augusta!

Date: 1825 Price: Exile Thought: Happy Families!

Super Big S Scoop triumph

TERRORIST HIDEOUT IN CATO STREET.

Vicious terrorist leaders were brought to book as they planned another cowardly and cruel attack on innocent victims.

FIENDISH PLAN TO KILL TORY CABINET!!!

Never before and never again could such a dastardly deed be contemplated! A group of bloodthirsty adulterers, fornicators, atheists, criminals and incestuous ne'er-do-wells, including Lord Byron, P.B. Shelley, and part-time scribbler W. Godwin, claimed that they HAD to eliminate the Tory government because it ruled solely for the benefit of the landed aristocracy and the rich.

THE BIG S SAYS: STRING THE SWINE UP!!!

Tory governments always have and always will rule only for their own benefit, and nobody has ever complained before!

THE ROCKET: 2 TO 1 FAVOURITE FOR THE DERBY

We're only joking, folks, but there is some nutter among our Northern brethren who has laid a few bob on this old nag to win! It will, he says, eat coal and gallop along at 15 miles per hour without getting tired!! It sounds to us more like the stuff real horses leave behind and which is very good for the roses!!!

The Big S says: Keep taking the tablets, George!

GREAT LOONIES OF OUR TIME: WILLIE WILBERFORCE

SLAVERY TO BE ABOLISHED!

Yes, Wee Willie is trotting out the same tired arguments again!

The Big S says: He's harmless, bless his little cotton socks!

And you'd better buy a pair quickly, because if there ain't no slaves, there ain't no cotton, and where would we be then, Willie?

SUPER FUN BIG S KRAZY KRAZE SUPER YOYO OFFER

Yes, folks, super FUN with our exclusive Big S YOYO.

Be the first in your hovel to have one!

Impress the girlies! Get a better job!

The world can be your oyster! **See details on page 7**

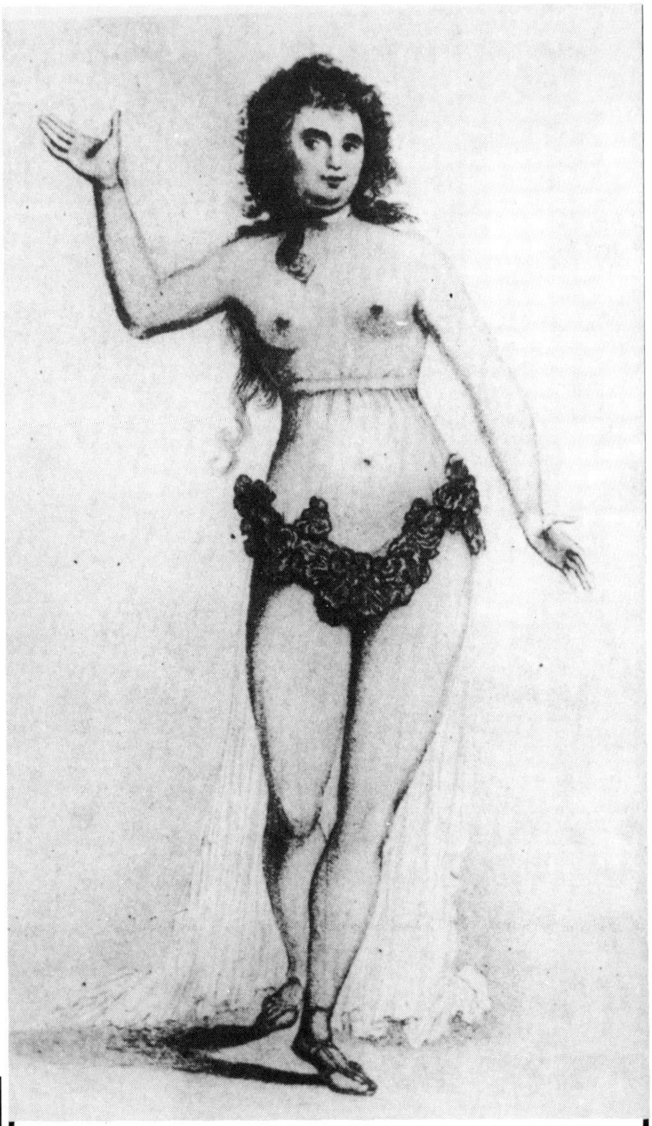

THEY TELL US THAT THIS LITTLE HIGH SOCIETY MISS HAS A PENCHANT FOR **FANCY DRESS BALLS**! WE'RE NOT SURPRISED: SHE'S A PRETTY SNAPPY DRESSER HERSELF.

INCEST IN SURREY!

Read the full details in the Big S NOW!

LORD'S SIS IN SECRET SEX SCANDAL

KISS-AND-DON'T-TELL-SISTER NOW TELLS THE BIG S THE SAUCY SECRETS OF LIFE AT HOME WITH BONK-MAD BARONET BYRON.

THE BIG S

ROYAL FASHION TIPS

Please, Ma'am
Do tidy yourself up a bit!
Bombasine is for the birds.
You and Albert look as if you belong in a Museum!

Date:1859 Price: Most of the world Thought: The Big S never sets.

The Big S says:
Don't worry, ma'am.
That's why we've got gunboats.
Just go out there and smash the bastards and jump up and down shouting "Gotcha! Gotcha! Gotcha!".

VIC'S

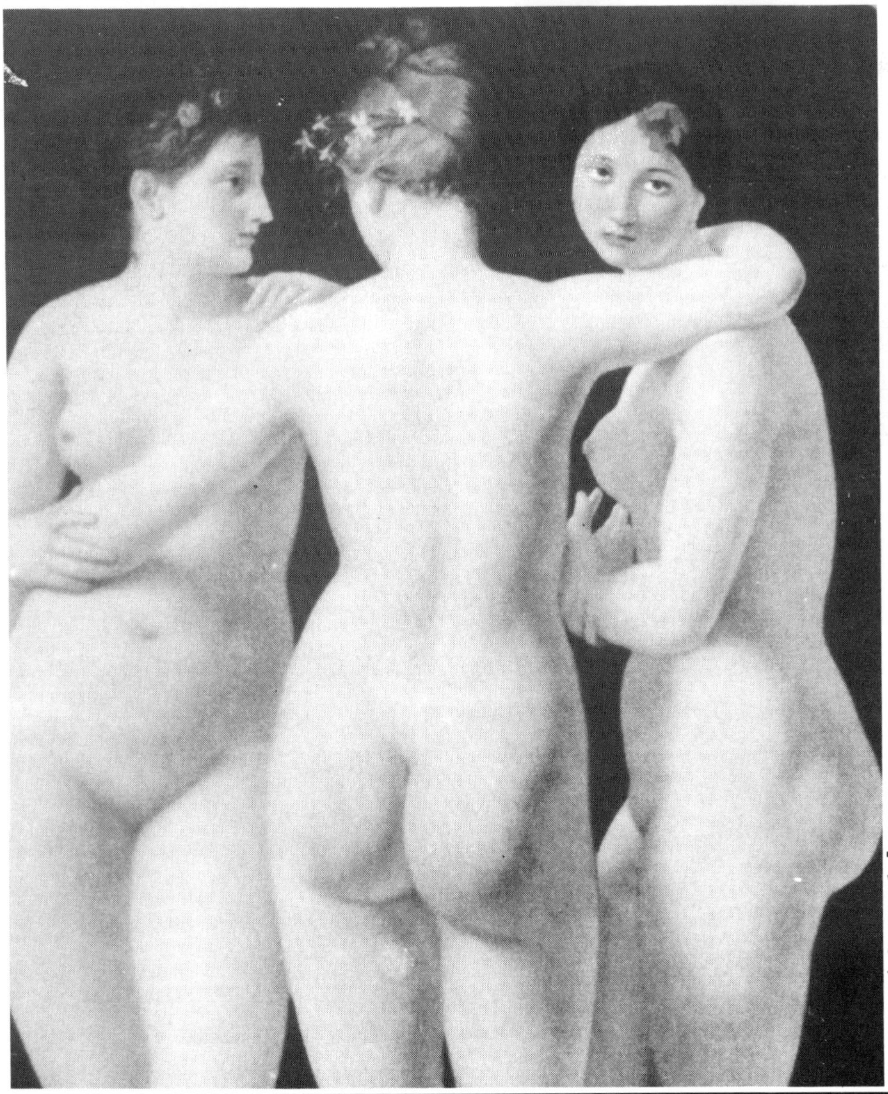

"AREN'T YOU THAT GEEZER, YOU KNOW, THE FELLOW WHO GOT LOST, DR WHAT'S-HIS-NAME?"

With those eloquent words which will echo down the ages, Stanley strolled up to old who's-his-face in the darkest jungle.

Now a nation can breathe again. Their dearly beloved, famous, intrepid explorer, Dr What-d'you-call-him, is safe and making great progress in civilising the black man. He told our special reporter that they haven't yet mastered all the intricacies of the leg break, they make a frightful cup of tea, and their spoken Latin, well, without being vulgar

(continued on page 9)

GREAT LOONIES OF OUR TIMES

Read about the crazy American who spends all his time digging holes in his garden. He says he's looking for something to make candles from!!!

Sounds as if he's too well-oiled already!

WE WARNED THEM WHAT WOULD HAPPEN IF THEY WENT THEIR OWN WAY!

Well, fellas, these three cheeky monkies don't look like apes to me!!! Mind you, I could go ape over three evolved little numbers like these!!! And although we would select these little cuties quite naturally, we still think Charlie Darwin should go back to his books and try again.

Super Fun Big S-clusive Super Special Royal Interview

BIG V TELLS IT THE WAY IT IS

FOREIGN POLICY - CHILD LABOUR

AND, FOR OUR READERS, A LOVELY PATTERN FOR BAGGY BLACK FROCKS!

IN AN EXCLUSIVE INTERVIEW OUR GRACIOUS QUEEN SPOKE ABOUT THE CARES, THE DUTIES AND THE JOYS OF BEING A MOTHER, A WIFE, AN EMPRESS AND A DEFENDER OF THE FAITH.

Her little dalliance with Froggie Emperor Nap the Third has got poor Vickie in a right royal tizzy!

KNICKS IN A TWIST

"Come in, darling," said Her Majesty to our special correspondent, "I'll tell you about foreign policy first, and then we can have a really good natter about girls' things afterwards. Are you kneeling comfortably? Good. Then I'll begin."

"First there was the Crimean War. That was all right because the old Ruskies had been asking for it for ages, and we didn't really need the Light Brigade any longer and we managed to make a few bob on the side."

"Then there was China, and that was all right because they're yellow and a hell of a long way away. Old Bony should have shared out Indo-China instead of grabbing it all for himself, but we managed to make a few bob anyway."

"But now there's Italy and Austria, and that's terribly complicated. If you only knew how much sleep I'm losing over all this. I mean to say, did Sardinia join the Crimean War just to curry favour in its struggle against Austria? If Sardinia does get the Austrians out of Italy, what's in it for old Bony? Will the conquest of the Papal States antagonise the Catholic bourgeoisie in France, and weaken his internal position, or will he be able to pinch a few choice bits for himself? Savoy and Nice would be nice and would tidy up the map a bit. But what about the Bourbons in Sicily? Would their reign be jeopardised? And what about the French advance in Africa, and those insane plans to conquer central America and the Hohenzollerns' intentions in Spain, and how can we manage to make a few bob out of all that? It never used to be that difficult in the good old days. You just sent the boats out and they beat up any dirty foreigner they came across."

A NICE CUP OF TEA

Then she smiled. "But enough of all that. Albert," she called out to the kitchen, "be a darling and put the kettle on. Now," she said, pulling her throne a little closer, "I must tell you about some absolutely lovely bombasine I found at the Market. As you know, Albert is really turned on by big

(continued on page 7)

THE BIG S

General Custer
is still standing.

For relief use Preparation How!

See advertisement on this page

Date: 1867 Price: One dollar Thought: You should listen to your elders and betters

SERVES YOU RIGHT - WE TOLD YOU

Next they'll come creeping and crawling back with their tails between their legs asking if they can be English again, please!

We said it at the time: Let them have a go and they'll soon find out.

FINE WORDS BUTTER NO PARSNIPS!!!

So all men are created equal, you said, but now you know that some are more equal than others, **and that those that don't agree with you aren't equal at all.**

A MOST UNCIVIL WAR

Now they're at it hammer and tongs again. This time all the white people in the North shooting all the white people in the South to decide whether black people are equal or not. What with this war and that war and Mexico and

(continued on page 7)

DIZZY IN A TIZZY!
DISRAELI DERAILED!

The Prime Minister has come up with an insane proposal to give workers the vote!

**The Big S says:
Knock it off, Big Ben! It'll be women next.**

They was robbed! Americans buy Alaska!

Serves you right again! We told you so!

Can you imagine it? $3000 dollars for Alaska! The old Ruskies must be laughing into their samovars tonight! Half a million square miles of snow and ice! I wonder what they think they're going to do with it.
They are just compulsive spenders! First they buy Louisiana! Then it's New Mexico and California! They'll splash out on any dodgy bit of real estate going!

I wonder if we could interest them in Millwall!!!

A MOST UNCIVIL WAR

This little lady looks a lot more equal than most to us! We wouldn't mind pursuing a bit of happiness with her, either up North or way down South.

THE BIG S

WHAT A LOAD OF JUNKERS

Date: 1871 Price: One Mark Thought: Sorry, cousin Wilhelm, but this time we are amused.

Can you cancan?

We jolly well could could with a saucy little numero like this, couldn't couldn't we, fellas?

SUPER FUN BIG S KRAZY KRAUT SCIENCE S-PLEMENT

Great loonies of our times.

HE'S THE SECOND CRAZY OTTO THIS WEEK!!!

We thought the penny-farthing was as weird as you could get, but we reckoned without crazy Otto!!!

He has invented, so he says, **a cycle with no wheels, and which catches fire as soon as it starts!**

The Big S says: Nice one, Otto, but take it a bit easy on the schnapps, and perhaps you wouldn't be so Blotto, Otto!!

SUPER FUN BIG S RELIGIOUS AFFAIRS S-PLEMENT

Overheard at the Vatican this week:
Cardinal (to Pope): Guess what, Pope, you're now infallible.
Pope (surprised): Get away with you! I'm sure you're wrong!

SUPER FUN BIG S ROYAL AFFAIRS S-PLEMENT

WHERE IS JOHN BROWN'S BODY LYING A-SMOULDERING TONIGHT?

VAT A BIG VILLY!

And that's official!

Old Kaiser Wilhelm of Prussia had himself officially declared an even bigger Willy today when he was made German Emperor in a ceremony held at Versailles.

All the Krauts were celebrating having given the Froggies a thorough-going thrashing in record time.

So it's **Bye-bye Bonaparte**, who's taking early retirement in Chislehurst, and **Hello Willy!!**

But now Willy wants to catch up with cousin Vickie: Willy wants an Empire!!!

So they've gone and stuck all their silly little states together, along with Alsace and Lorraine and a few other miserable little bits they've pinched, and they're calling that the German Empire! I wonder if they'd like Millwall as well!

And old Otto von Bismarck, a true Prussian Bue if ever there was one, was busy snatching up the scraps round his master's table: now he's decided that he's a Prince!

BIG S ART S-PLEMENT

New art sensation sweeps Paris. Manet says he paints only what he sees. The Big S says: Either you get to better picnics than we do, Edouard, or you've bought some very dodgy specs!!!

THE BIG S

Date: 1900 Price:Too much Thought: Who controls the past controls the future

It's all Scouts today!

Buffalo Bill had the good idea of giving up scouting in the Wild West to scout out little treasures like this one, currently appearing right here in town at BUFFALO BILL'S CIRCUS.

SOME MAMMAS DO 'AVE 'EM!!

Poor Mrs Marconi. Her little boy, Giuglielmo, he used to be so good. He could have done anything he wanted: he could have made the ice-cream, been an opera singer or a great gangster! And married a nice girl! And had lotsa bambini!

And now what does he do?

He sits all day with a little box, tapping out noises by knocking two little bitsa metal together!!! He says he has to know if anybody can hear him!!!

"We all tell him," his mamma cried to our reporter, "all the family, we say 'Giuglielmo, we hear you. We're right here. We hear you.' But does he listen? Povero! He says 'You don't-a understand, Mamma. It's the man across the sea who should hear me!' And Uncle Luigi, he say, 'Don't-a worry, Esmeralda. We take him to see-a somebody. My wife's cousin has a friend who is a doctor.

(continued on page 9)

German inventor round the Benz

Kraut invents a **horseless carriage!** And he must have been legless at the time! He should get together with crazy Otto who has a cycle with no wheels on it.

These foreign loonies have a knack of inventing means of transport that they've forgotten to put the means of transport in.

Next we'll have the Eyeties trying to sail round the world in a gravy boat!!!!

POO! WHAT A PONK!

Prince of Wales has a sniff at Froggie flatulence!

Oh la la! It's gay Paree! We've already heard of so-called artists, little midgets painting pictures of prostitutes for adverts! We've already heard of so-called musicians, writing music for ladies who jump around and show their knickers.

FROGGIES FLOCK TO THE MUSICAL F*RTER

Everybody is fighting to see a young man who can whistle and hum catchy tunes from that end of the body usually unassociated with such voluntary and controlled exhalations.

Even the charms of feminine pulchritude so amply displayed on the Parisian stages are being forgotten as people from all walks of life rush to hear this latest musical instrument, both the most natural and the most unnatural you might ever come across.

The pinnacle of the young musician's career must have been yesterday when he gave a private performance for the Prince of Wales and a few chosen friends.

The Big S says: By Appointment to His Majesty, purveyor of flatulence! Keep it up, Edward! It's nice to know the taxes are being so well spent!

PHEW! WHAT A RELIEF

We're glad to see that all those little badges did come in useful after all.

Yes, Lord Baden-Powell, well-known soldier and admirer of short trousers, has fully deserved his **"holding-out-for-the-sake-of-Queen-and-country-when-under-siege-in-some-God-forsaken-hole-that-nobody-in-his-right-mind-would-fight-about-anyway" badge.**

Mafeking has been relieved, and those nasty boring Boers have been sent packing.

PHEW! WHAT A RELIEF!

The little lovely on this relief must have been pretty relieved to find she had a couple of helping hands to assist with her underwear.

We don't really understand the differences between bas-relief and high-relief, but we reckon that this is a pretty Eye-Eye-relief!

We wouldn't mind relieving a little beauty like this, would we, fellas?

THE BIG S

Come back, Icarus. All is forgiven.

Date: The twentieth century | Price: Who knows? | Thought: Per ardua ad astra?

READ THE BIG S NEXT WEEK AND EVERY WEEK IN THE NEW SUPER BIG S SPECIAL S-CLUSIVE CENTURY

Place an order now, and get all the answers to the exciting questions in our super fun BIG S Twentieth Century Quiz!

Will the Tsar ever get rid of Rasputin?

Will Coventry City finally win the Cup?

Will the horseless carriage finally be banned?

Will universal male suffrage ever be pushed through?

Will 5904 years of ROYAL brown-nosing finally get RM the honour he so richly doesn't deserve? Will he be Lord Rudepratt of Wapping?

Will Victoria go on for ever?

Will RM buy out the remainder of Big G's holdings? Or will he take the money and run?

Will the wireless telegraph always be engaged?

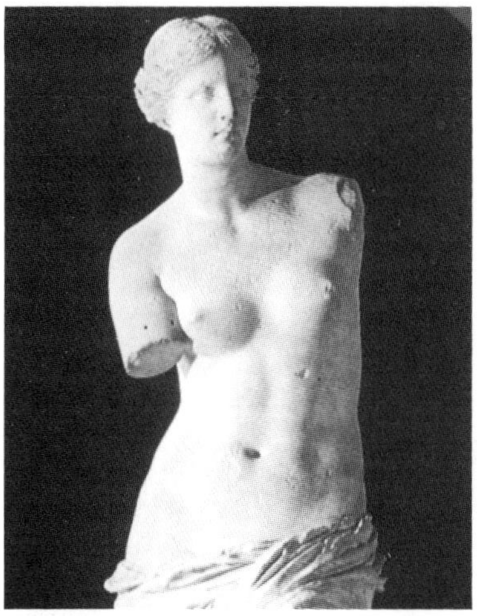

Assuming that they do get round to creating it, will the National Health Service be safe in their hands? or will this little lovely still be on a waiting list?

Will breasts be in or out?

Will bustles still be big?

Will we really have a woman Prime Minister?

SUPER BIG S NEW CENTURY COMPETITION
Find a use for the heavier-than-air flying machine

AIR WE GO FOLKS!

WRIGHTS OFF THEIR ROCKERS!

HOW MANY MORE TIMES DO WE HAVE TO SAY THAT WE TOLD THEM SO?

Two brothers in America have spent a fortune trying to invent a flying machine. They have spent more than $25000 to build a contraption 50 feet wide and 30 feet long. And don't laugh, readers, it's a shame really, but it's got pedals and a motor that is supposed to lift itself off the ground and fly through the air for up to 50 feet!!!

The Big S says:
Pigs have more chance of flying than you two loony-tunes!

Mind you, if they did manage it, they'd have a very bright future. People would be queuing up to buy a machine 50 foot long and 30 foot high that jumps up and down!!

Very rich people could use it for getting across puddles in the street, but they'll have to make the pavements a bit wider to get the machine in. Or you could use it when you've dug the garden and don't want to walk back across the part you've dug. Or when you've washed the kitchen floor and are stuck in the far corner when that other great new invention, the telephone, rings!!! Or for cleaning the upstairs windows! or sweeping the

(continued on page 7)

THE BIG S

BIG S SUPER FUN ILLUSTRATED HISTORY OF THE WORLD SUPER FUN COMPETITION

Date: Today Price: Cheap at twice the price Thought: The Big S breaks through the darkest clouds

WIN A MILLION

YES, A MILLION COULD BE YOURS!

A **MILLION** grains of sand, one to represent **EVERY SINGLE YEAR OF HISTORY** from the Lower Palaeolithic Age to **THIS VERY MOMENT!!!**

ALL HUMAN HISTORY CAN BE YOURS!!!

Yes, readers, why not put **YOUR MILLION** in an attractive, washable, easy-care,clear plastic box -available from **THE BIG S** at a silly price- and stand it on top of the television set???
YOUR FRIENDS AND NEIGHBOURS will admire it and **ADMIRE YOU!!!** It will be a never-failing subject of lively and witty conversation, and once you have, **IN THE PRIVACY OF YOUR VERY OWN HOME,** this **EXCLUSIVELY CHOSEN, LIMITED EDITION MONUMENT** to **ALL HUMAN HISTORY -although for legal reasons we are not allowed to make any definite promises-** you will almost **CERTAINLY** find that the **GIRLIES** are much more willing to

(continued on page 101)

HERE'S WHAT YOU HAVE TO DO

Now that you've read this book carefully, think about the qualities of the hundreds of inspiring LEADERS, WARRIORS, KINGS, SCIENTISTS, MEN OF LETTERS, INVENTORS, EXPLORERS, POETS, PAINTERS, POLITICIANS and RELIGIOUS LEADERS brought to you in these pages. Then look at the list below and put the qualities in order of importance for your **IDEAL WORLD LEADER!!!**

For example, if you think that **Characteristic B: Compassion** is the most important, then write **B1** on a postcard. If you think **Characteristic D: Honesty** is the second most important, then write **D2** underneath B1. Carry on until you have put all the characteristics in order.

A: LEARNING **B: COMPASSION** **C: SENSE OF HUMOUR**
D: HONESTY **E: INTELLIGENCE** **F: A REALLY NICE PAIR**
G: PERSISTENCE **H: UNDERSTANDING**

If you manage to relate these characteristics to any of the people mentioned in this book -except for Quality F- then you might as well go out and shoot yourself as an incurable fool!

No, seriously, folks, when you have listed the characteristics in your order of importance, AS A TIE BREAKER, write a sentence of NOT MORE THAN TWENTY WORDS on: Is culture born of civilisation, or civilisation of culture?

Answers on a postcard please BEFORE THE END OF THE CENTURY.

The judges' decision is final. No correspondence will be entered into, except about quality F, if appropriate and accompanied by photographic evidence.